Astrology of Health

Physical and Psychological

Health

in the

Natal and

Progressed Charts

Noel Eastwood

IMPORTANT LEGAL NOTICE

This book is intended to give the student of astrology insight into the health indicators of the astrological chart or horoscope. It is stressed that the contents of this book are in no way a substitute for personal health supervision by a qualified medical professional. This book is not intended to provide medical diagnosis nor is it a substitute for professional medical treatment. If you have a health condition you are directed to seek professional medical help.

To protect the privacy of certain individuals mentioned in this book their names and identifying details have been changed. You will also note that their birth details have been deleted for this same purpose.

This book is copyrighted. Apart from any fair use for the purposes of private study, research, criticism or review as permitted by the Copyright Act, no part may be reproduced without written permission of the author.

WARNING: always seek professional medical advice for health complaints.

Inquiries should be addressed to: Noel Eastwood:

Web site: www.plutoscave.com

Email: info@plutoscave.com

All rights reserved copyright © 2016 Noel Eastwood

Front cover: *Chiron, the Wounded Healer* - Illustrator James, Cloud Pillow Studio - cloudpillowstudio@gmail.com

Dedication: This book is dedicated to my students and clients who taught me so much. A special thank you goes to my dear brother Mark Eastwood for taking the time to assist in proof reading this book. To my good friend, astrologer and philosopher, Maria Pocsai-Faglin, thank you once again for your support and help in editing, formatting and preparing for publication.

Table of Contents

Preface

Introduction

Chapter 1: Elements as Defenses

Chapter 2: Air Dominance in Health

Chapter 3: Fire Dominance in Health

Chapter 4: Water Dominance in Health

Chapter 5: Constitutional health - Part 1 - Planets

Chapter 6: Constitutional health - Part 2 - Signs and Houses

Chapter 7: Focusing on the whole chart - heredity, Bach remedies, homeopathy, meditating on astrological archetypes for health

Chapter 8: Triggers or Indicators of illness through Transit, Direction and Progression

Chapter 9: Operations - timing an operation, healing miracles, astrological archetypes in meditation

Appendix 1: Common Defence Mechanisms

Appendix 2: Article: Miracle Healing

Appendix 3: Article: Amazing Experiences In Trance with the astrological Archetypes

Appendix 4: Inflammation and the Four Elements

Appendix 5: Recommended Reading List

Appendix 6: Inflammatory Illness

About Noel Eastwood and Pluto's Cave

Preface

This book is the result of a lifetime of personal experience and research as an astrologer, healer and psychotherapist. Initially I created this as an online course quite some years ago. I was so inspired by the feedback from students that I transcribed and condensed the notes and conversations for this book. This was a work of love and one that I now pass on to those astrologers and healers who wish to know a little more of the link between astrology and health. As a psychotherapist I have tried to tone down my bias towards psychological health in the charts, but as a healer I recognise just how important the link between mind and body truly is. I am quite sure that this approach and the lively conversation format will both entertain and enlighten you.

Introduction

No traditionally trained Tibetan healer would make up a herbal prescription for a patient without first drawing up their astrological charts. It was the same back in the Middle Ages in European culture: astrology and medicine were one. When my good friend and healer, Harald Tietze, was invited to speak with the Dalai Lama in Tibet, he was fascinated by how thorough traditional Tibetan medical training was.

The five year Degree in Traditional Tibetan Medicine or the Degree of Traditional Tibetan Astrology, was required before a healer was allowed to practice. Thirty percent of the staff at the Tibetan Medical & Astrological Institute of His Holiness the Dalai Lama of Dharamsala were involved solely in the preparation of astrological charts. A patient's natal chart is still used for initial diagnosis and in determining the best medical remedies and treatment.

Candy Hillenbrand, in her excellent article on Bach Remedies in the journal of Federation of Australian Astrologers (FAA) (Vol. 24, No. 4, 1994), affirms that our healer ancestors were also trained in reading the stars, they were astrologers. Paracelsus in the 16th century, as well as Nicholas Culpeper in the 17th century, wrote of the links between astrology, illness and its treatment. Culpeper once said: *"Only astrologers are fit to study medicine and a medical man without astrology is like a lamp without oil."*

Jane Bennett also discusses healing in her book, *A Handbook of Astrology for Australia and New Zealand*, (1986). She wrote that Ptolemy, author of *Tetrabiblios*, a third-century book incorporating astrology and medicine, thoroughly delineated (described) all the known Planets in terms of their health properties.

The famous Greek healer, Hippocrates, recognised as the Father of Medicine, taught astrology to his medical students for both diagnosis and to determine critical days in illness. He said: *"He who does not understand astrology is not a doctor but a fool."* By the Middle Ages astrology was an entrenched tool of medicine and taught at universities as a required course of study in medicine. Up until the 18th century it was not possible to qualify as a doctor without also being qualified in astrology in most universities.

The industrial and scientific revolution, along with the rise of fundamentalist Christianity, saw the demise of astrology as a viable and credible tool of medicine and healing. Today, astrology is considered either the devil's work or completely without value. It saw a resurgence in the second half of the 20th century but now, in the early days of the 21st Century, it remains a new age oddity.

Sadly, astrology is rarely recognised today for its value in gaining a better understanding of health. Astrology does, however, predate all other kinds of scientific health diagnosis. As a diagnostic tool astrologers can see their client's problems before they manifest and advise when to take precautions or suggest specific remedies when qualified to do so.

Michel Gauquelin, (author of *Planetary Heredity*, 1966 and 1988), used scientific methodology to show how the Planets affect our health and wellbeing. His research has done much to enhance our understanding of astrology, personality and health. Sadly, this struggle for recognition of his life work took its toll and he died prematurely in 1991.

Reinhold Ebertin (1901-1988) also made an enormous contribution to medical astrology by presenting astrological medicine using accepted scientific modeling. His research was always well presented and highly professional (read his *The Combination of Stellar Influences*). Ebertin systematically studied heart attack victims and kidney disorders then presented papers explaining his findings. By eliminating esoteric translations from his astrological work, he was widely accepted by many scientists and astrologers alike.

Jane Bennett (author of *A Handbook of Astrology or Australia & New Zealand*, 1986), also explored the role of astrology in healing. She asked a number of astrologers / natural therapists how they used astrology in their practice. She noted that all the therapists she spoke to used medical astrology and were knowledgeable about the psychological application of astrology. *"The greater depth of psychological understanding gives the practitioner access to the deeper levels from where the illness or disease originally emerged."* (ibid, p.60).

Astrologer and natural therapist Peter Berryman, said, *"Healing is most concerned with mental, emotional and spiritual health, as the physical body is the end product of imbalance in these areas."* (ibid, p. 61).

Naturopath, Sally Gillespie says, *"I find having the client's chart in front of me speeds up diagnosis considerably. Where it helps me is in diagnosing where people are out of balance in their whole system, which provides the necessary grounds for illness, as well as seeing, through Transits and Progressions, what particular stresses are on them at the moment. Generally, it's pretty obvious in which part of the body the stress is manifesting itself, but when it's not, the whole chart can point to the most likely areas to look into."*

Always seek professional medical advice for any health complaints, particularly with children.

Chapter 1

Elements as Defenses

The Elements help explain the connections between physical and psychological health. We develop defenses to protect our very sensitive emotions. They provide the necessary barriers to the harsh realities of the world. Defenses are necessary, but if they become too well developed they become a problem. We tend to withdraw behind these defensive barriers which, unfortunately, prevent us from fully participating in the world around us.

We see defenses in the chart when an Element dominates the chart through the placement of: Planets, Signs, Houses, Ascendant and chart Signature.

Not everyone will have a single dominant Element, often there are two, but we all have defenses. No-one is free of them. We look at Planets in their Elements, the chart Signature, Final Dispositors, House emphasis, Ascendant Element, the Element of the most aspected Planet, Planets conjunct the Luminaries, Planets on the Angles, Planet of High Degree, etc. These points in the chart are the keys that highlight your Elemental dominance and thus your defenses. Defenses also work in closely with Carl Jung's Complexes and Projections.

Astrologers also examine a chart for Elemental deficits or weaknesses. For instance, when the Air Element is extremely weak it forms complexity in defence formation. An Air deficit may contribute to the native having less intellectual flexibility. This means that the native tends to adapt and use other Elemental modalities to communicate. Deficits need to be considered in context of the entire chart.

Using a holistic approach to health, we can conclude that whatever makes us physically unwell will also make us psychologically unwell. It also suggests that psychological problems will also manifest as physical problems. This simply says: "when we are stressed we get sick". It forms a cycle.

Our thoughts affect how we feel. In the long term repression in one direction tends to force a weakness in another. For instance, worry can create headaches, but having a headache can make us worry. An example is depression, which can be a product of both physical and psychological ill health.

Earth Dominance in Health

Earth dominant people defend against the insecurity of change by exerting control over their possessions and physical environment. They manage their insecurities by hoarding and collecting, they find comfort in controlling and stabilising their environment. Sameness is comfortable, change is frightening. They struggle against authority figures who try to take control of their possessions or their feelings.

According to Dr Sigmund Freud, the Father of Psychoanalysis, this is the 'Psychosexual' or psychological defence that develops around the time of toilet training. Freud puts this stage at around the time when the child discovers that they can control their flow of urine and faeces. The issue is one of regulating their pleasurable physical experiences.

When the child discovers that they can control their world they also want to want to do the same with their toileting. But no, now an authority figure takes control and claims the product of the child's pleasure, faeces. This can set up a power conflict between authority (mother, father or nanny) and the child.

When someone becomes fixated at this psychosexual stage, the Earth defence becomes a power conflict with anyone in authority who tries to remove the native's control over their pleasure-giving possessions. This resistance is projected onto the school teacher, police, neighbour and anyone else who tells them what to do and when to do it.

The Earth dominant native is in charge of everything that brings pleasure, be it the toilet, bath, playing with toys or having fun with their friends. As they grow older they control and collect other gratifying things such as money, houses, cars, businesses, partners, lovers, etc.

This Earth dominance can become destructive when they fall in love and start dating. The Earth person starts to oversee the giving and withholding of another crucial product: affection. They do this by controlling their loved one's access to house money, work contacts, schedule , shopping, access to the TV, computer, internet or phone and by limiting their partner's access to their friends and family. This creates a battleground in the marriage and I will often see the loser of this power struggle in my counseling clinic.

Earth strengths include the incredible stamina to work on a task, no matter how challenging it may be. Think of those postmen who set out to do their job be it rain, hail or sunshine. When something involves perseverance, it is those with a strong Earth Element who will stick till it's done. They are reliable, resourceful and dependable in their desire to complete a task with maximum efficiency.

Earth dominance is seen with the Luminaries in Earth Signs or Houses (2nd, 6th and 10th), and strongly placed Venus (particularly in Taurus), Saturn and Mercury (particularly in Virgo). For psychologists and counsellors, a Planetary Stellium in an Earth House will help you examine this defence fixations in therapy.

Other points to look for in an Earth dominance are aspects, particularly Conjunctions, to the Luminaries Sun and Moon. For instance, Mercury conjunct Moon in Virgo will give an earthy emotional reaction. Saturn conjunct Sun or Moon is an extremely earthing Conjunction that could build and strengthen self esteem.

Earth Planets on the Angles, such as Saturn conjunct the Ascendant, are extremely powerful. So too is Saturn in an Earth House (2nd, 6th or 10th House). Difficulties can arise with Venus and Mercury, as they play a dual role in astrological rulerships. Venus rules both Taurus (is passive in Earth Signs) and Libra (is active in Air Signs). Mercury rules both Gemini (is active in Air Signs) and Virgo (is passive in Earth Signs). We would look at the whole chart to see if these Planets are in an active or passive state when determining Elemental dominance.

Saturn is the earthiest of the Planets He rules Capricorn and as such is extremely domineering and controlling of all our Earthly pleasures. Saturn may not enjoy them but he certainly will control them.

We also look for Stelliums in Earth Signs (Taurus, Virgo and Capricorn) and in Earth Houses (2nd, 6th and 10th). A Grand Cross is considered to be an Earth Planetary pattern. It has the power to contain and control the urges and instincts of the native. It is like a castle, complete with moat and walls and helps the native control the external stressors from penetrating their softer emotional centre. But it might also stop them enjoying a lot of the pleasures and freedom of being in love or just participating in the fun of life.

In regards to health issues, hoarding can lead to a buildup of toxins in the body. 'Constipation' is a health term we can substitute for 'Hoarding'. Problems arise when food is held in the intestines for too long, a result of the earthy impulse to 'hold on', a form of control. Earth Signs learn that they can help remove these toxins by sharing their belongings and emotions, a good diet and some exercise.

Another facet of Earth is skeletal structure and teeth. We would try to identify the powerful Elements of Saturn and Capricorn here. Saturn however, is not always a sure-fire Significator for skeletal or tooth problems, so we would have to consider a Stellium in Capricorn and/or the 10th House. Stating that someone will have problems in this area because of a poorly aspected Saturn is way too general. That's why we always have a look at other factors.

I would consider a poorly placed Saturn and a Stellium in the 10th House or Capricorn, for bone issues, only if the native is pregnant, seeking to fall pregnant or already have weak bones. We try to advise wisely without frightening people, so people susceptible to breaks and osteoporosis can be warned appropriately.

My earthy friend, Laurie, who has a strong Earth emphasis in his chart, came home broken in body and spirit at the end of the war. After a lifetime of self-abuse, cigarettes, alcohol and shattered self-esteem, he was ready for the morgue. But Laurie was tough, he wouldn't let lymphatic cancer, pacemaker, nil circulation in his legs, skin cancers, blocked arteries in his neck and a stroke (not to mention the numerous panic attacks and tropical diseases) stop him from living.

On one of his down days Laurie read Ross Horne's book, *Improving on Pritikin*. He decided to give it a go, it couldn't harm him, he was already dying. Eating only fruit for the next two and a half years gave him back his life: his cancers disappeared; he had no need for his pacemaker; fresh blood circulated freely in his legs; he had no need for blood pressure tablets; he was free of the anxiety and the dark depths of depression that had plagued him since 1945.

Laurie was a living legend and demonstrated the healing power of raw fruit, vegetables and solid determination. I was honoured to have been there to assist in his psychological healing. He died at the ripe age of 82 years.

In summary: health problems can arise with an emphasis on Earth Planets, Signs and Houses. Look for 2nd, 6th or 10th House emphasis or Taurus, Virgo or Capricorn. Also consider Mercury, Venus and Saturn especially when the first two shared Planets are in Earth Signs. Saturn is the strongest of the Earth Planets and is the best indicator of control, domination, power struggles and toxaemia.

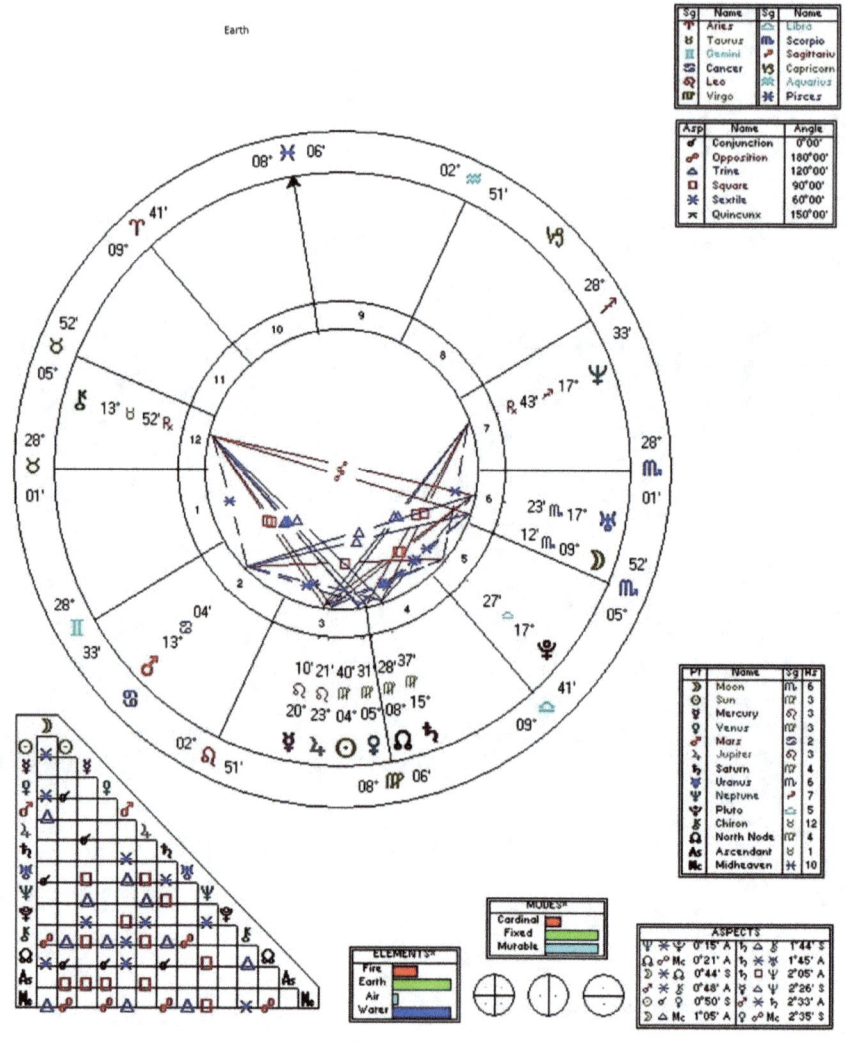

Lesson 1

Noel: *Welcome to this course and as you have found out it is very hard to find information on astrology and healing.*

Student: Well, the historical stuff is difficult to find on the web. In a decent library it would be a different matter.

- True, early astrologers sought to find systems to best understand the complicated human system of health.

N - I don't care if the system isn't simple. I just want it to be reliable and to be something I can learn. I am planning to start consulting as an astrologer.

S - Good on you. Becoming a professional astrologer is hard work. It requires a lot of patience, I have a day job as a psychologist, teach astrology, Taoist meditation, tai chi and chi healing so I suggest that you have other options for income.

N - Do you know the book 'Nourishing Destiny' by Lonny Jarrett?

S - No...

N - It's about the philosophy of Chinese medicine. An acupuncturist recommended it to me.

S - OK, we might look into Chinese medicine later, it is an interest of mine too. In your lesson notes, I mentioned other astrologers who used healing techniques along with astrology. It seems that people have been working on creating their own systems to combine ancient wisdom and modern theories of health diagnosis and symptomology. We know so much more than our ancestors did about the human body, causes and symptoms. Now we are seeking to integrate this with what today's astrologers have found. They combine both using a modern approach. In other words, we don't try to copy ancient texts word for word. They are not as accurate as we would like them to be. Not that we are rudely tossing their knowledge out. We aim to refine, enhance and build upon their original work. I like to introduce the four Elements, Earth, Air, Fire and Water, as powerful forces in our charts. Just as Liz Greene, Stephen Arroyo and other modern astrologers have demonstrated and as I have found in my own practice, the Elements are extremely powerful. Now to look at Psychological Defences, even though I am not teaching psychology in this series of lessons, we do recognise that physical illness often parallels our mental and emotional states. The psychological defences are now interpreted as both psychological and physical: psychosomatic. Earth, the Element of control, is a very powerful defence. Why? Because it holds on to things. OK, do you have some Earth key words?

S - Order...practicality...societal expectations...productivity.

N - Great. We note that society is also seen in the Moon, Cancer and the North Node, which would be particularly emphasised if in an Earth Sign. When we think in terms of health we look at the conflict. This is a brilliant way to read a chart. Please go to the **Earth chart** in this lesson. Let's begin by looking for the conflict in this chart. Look at the Houses first, are the Earth Houses, 2, 6 and 10 involved?

S - Mars (Square to Pluto) is in the 2nd House. There is a Moon-Uranus conjunct in the 6th opposing Chiron (ouch).

N - Quite important. It is in Scorpio, too. Straight away we see the conflict in the person's psyche. When we have conflict we have the person's motivations. Their most important life decisions revolve around this conflict. Mother issues (Moon), tension, stress (Uranus), wounded (Chiron Opposition) and health (6th House). What else is there in the chart to show tension, stress, wounds, etc. that might affect health?

S - There are three Virgo Planets. Virgo suggests sensitivity, over conscientiousness, self-criticism... It's the anxious Earth Sign.

N - Yes and they are clustered around an Angle, the 4th House cusp, makes them very strong, always willing to serve, especially easy to frighten.

S - There is also the Saturn-Neptune Square and I guess there is a Fixed T-Square with Chiron, Uranus, and Mercury. More strain on the nervous system.

N - Yes this is generational so we must consider it in light of affecting the entire cohort born with this pattern. The T-Square throws stress at Mercury which is nervousness. What we are seeing here is that even without the Virgo Stellium on an Angle the person is a very complicated entity. They have many issues and forces driving them. There are many things that will influence health not just their 6th House. It just so happens that this person has a major conflict in their 6th House of health. But what about *people who have nothing in their 6th? If someone has nothing in the 6th House what do we look for to see their health properties?*

S - Aspects to the Ascendant or the Ascendant ruler. Placement and aspects to the ruler of the 12th. Hard aspects especially to the Moon.

N - Good. When a person has 'conflict' they tend to focus their lives aimed at resolving it. Thus energy is drawn towards and away from organs, muscles, etc. The things you just noted all point to the importance of finding conflict in their lives. The Moon, Ascendant and the 12th House cusp are all major centres of emotion and vulnerable to stress. Stress contributes to ill health. The natal chart points to birth or constitutional health and what we bring into this life and the weaknesses we are born with. To find them we look for conflict which includes the most aspected Planet and Planets conjunct the Ascendant or the 12th cusp or the Moon. Patterns: T-Squares, Grand Crosses, Inner Planets conjunct Outer Planets[1]. All are major stresses in our life.

The major stresses in this chart are: Moon conjunct Uranus in Scorpio in the 6th House. The person defends against emotional blackmail, jealousy and domestic violence. Thus for most of their life they guard against these conflicts. A good defence against emotional blackmail and aggression and vulnerability is, in this particular individual's case, an Earth defence. So, how does a person apply Earth defences?

S - You mean this person specifically?

N - Yes, but generally too.

S - Emotional withholding. Withholding help or aid.

N - Yes. By holding back their love and affection too, they are less vulnerable and they begin to control their partner. A very powerful defense. So the key words for Earth are withholding, control and power plays. When a person has a strong Earth chart they are very good at control through withholding their emotions and tightly managing their social interactions or relationships. But there is a side effect to this. What could that be in terms of health?

S - Stress builds up inside from repressed emotional needs.

N - Yes. And this leads to...?

S - Disease

N - Yes. Where?

S - Toxic colon

N - Perfect. The elimination system which Virgo controls through service - how? They stop running around serving others and they stop giving.

S - The colon is ruled by Scorpio, a Water Sign.

N - Yes, our traditional rulerships apply as well. We are applying new information, new findings and seeing how they can be brought together. I see Scorpio ruling the sexual energy as well as elimination.

S - Okay, then I'll hold that thought 'til we go over the Signs.

N - You may find that some of what is presented here is not in line with traditional astrology. We always consider the chart holistically, as bit by bit does not work. We are not bits and pieces, we are whole human beings and very complicated. The Earth Planets: Saturn, Mercury (in Virgo) and Venus (in Taurus). The Signs are: Virgo, Taurus and Capricorn. That is basic astrology of course but what do they stand for and represent? Taureans prefer to act. They are solid and hard-working and when they get upset they stop working. They withhold. Virgoans of course, stop serving and Capricornians stop giving or following orders.

S - What you're presenting is very interesting and controversial in some ways because I know of a woman with an Earth-heavy chart who died of colon cancer at age 49. Organs of elimination, colon, rectum, kidneys, bladder, sweat glands, wastes, poisons, excess stuff.

N - And what happens when these toxins stop being eliminated?

S - You're in big trouble.

N - This reminds me of the joke about the body parts: They body parts had a meeting to decide who was the most important and should rule the human body. The eyes said they were because they could see things. The ears said that they were because they could hear things. The hands said that they were because they could hold things. After much arguing the anus stood up and said that he was the most important and should rule the human body. All of the other organs started to laugh! So he stopped doing what he does best, he stopped eliminating. After one day the eyes began to water. After two days the ears began to whistle. After three days the hands began to tremble. After four days the other body parts gave in and agreed that the Anus really ruled the human body.

S - I like that story, it sure fits.

N - So Earth defences are powerful and are also necessary to protect the individual, initially. The problem arises when the power struggle is over but the defence mechanism does not end. If it continues, it causes problems. Over the long term this defence begins to damage the system leading to ill health. In our Earth chart: Taurus Ascendant and a Virgo Stellium on the powerful 4th House cusp, both are Earth. Saturn is also on an Angle, the 4th. If we accept that the native is distressed emotionally by the Moon-Uranus-Chiron pattern, then we can accept that an Earth defence could well be activated to protect it.

But there is also a strong Water Element here too, we won't go into that in this lesson. However, it may be the activating component that triggers the Earth health problems that this person is experiencing.

S - Question. How do we know that Earth defenses will be used to protect the Water part of the person rather than Water defenses used to protect the Earth part of the person?

N - Good question, this shows just how complicated we are. No simple, single system of diagnosis works all the time and we should always consider every component in the chart. To answer your question we seek to locate the most powerful influences in the chart: Sun, Moon, Ascendant, MC and the three Inner Planets, Mercury, Venus and Mars. Moon is powerful with an Outer Planet Conjunction, Uranus. Sun is powerful conjunct Venus and North Node and it is part of a Stellium; Venus is powerful as Lord of the Chart; Mercury is powerful as ruler of the Sun Sign and Stellium and Mercury is also exalted in its own House. There is enough Earth there to slightly push aside the Water influence but only partly. This person, as you pointed out, is a combination of both these Elements. I will add that Air will also trigger some Air defences (such as denial) with that Moon conjunct Uranus and the Stellium in the 3rd House. This person will also use Water defences, and we should look at them if this person came for a reading, but their dominant Earth has visible health implications.

To find a chart that has only the single Elemental defence is very unusual. Really difficult.

S - So we'll be working our way through the Elements to start off?

N - Yes, each Element. Then we move along to apply it to the Signs, Planets and everything else in the chart. I will see you next lesson, take care.

Chart: Earth - the ELEMENTS grid at the bottom mid right, above the MODES, shows that Earth and Water dominate while Air is very weak. We note how Earth dominates with a Taurus Ascendant, Sun, Venus, North Node and Saturn in Virgo, and Chiron is in Taurus. That is six points in Earth. This includes the most powerful points: Sun and the Ascendant; followed by the Personal Planet Venus.

Water is also strong with another powerful point, Moon, which is in Scorpio. However, we must also consider that the Moon is in an Earth House, the 6th. In this instance, the Moon's Earth House placement contributes to the chart's overall Earth qualities.

We always consider the Planets, Signs and Houses holistically. This is why the Moon in Scorpio, a Water Planet in a Water Sign, also counts as an Earth point by its House placement, the 6th House. This chart has both Moon and Uranus in an Earth House and are counted as both Water (Moon + Scorpio), Air (Moon conjunct Uranus) and Earth (6th House).

Looking at the 3rd House Stellium we see how these Virgo Planets can contribute to elevating Air higher than what the ELEMENT grid of the astrological software indicates. Determining your client's elemental dominance is a vital first calculation in determining their health qualities. And, as you can see, it is not easy and takes practice.

Chapter 2

Air Dominance in Health

An Air dominance defends against excess emotion, reality, confusion, ambivalence and restriction on freedom of expression. It can easily deny that anything is wrong when situations become emotionally overwhelming. Often these natives will dissociate and escape into fantasy to avoid facing personal emotional issues. Air dominant people can come up with incredible intellectual explanations or resort to magical thinking to avoid facing their feelings. This is particularly evident in their management of intimate relationships.

Air dominance often seeks to adopt an intellectual mindset to avoid painful situations and they struggle to keep their cool in all circumstances. They may simply cut off their emotions preferring to engage solely with a conscious, rational mindset. They can have great difficulty expressing how they feel. Air dominance types are most comfortable talking about love and affection but they are not so comfortable experiencing or demonstrating it. They can appear quite cold.

The Air dominant person often presents for counselling stuck inside their head. These clients have great difficulty acknowledging and managing their feelings and become confused when confronted with emotional relationship and family dynamics. It is the Air types that I see most frequently in my practice, as they tend to think too much and to avoid their feelings. This becomes so powerful that it invades their everyday, conscious mind and can prevent them falling asleep at night. It is possibly the most common cause of stress and disturbed sleep in our culture.

One of the first questions I ask my clients is if they have 'racing negative thoughts'. Once this is identified, I help them disengage their busy conscious mind and direct them to talk about what is really going on in their lives. This involves a complex series of therapeutic processes including self hypnosis, guided meditation, deep relaxation and biofeedback (neurofeedback). Most of my work with Air types is listening, normalising and helping them examine their thinking processes and untangling their confused emotions.

Air dominance types can be difficult to treat but they respond very well to the above strategies once they realise it will help. The first part of their therapy is to convince them to participate with their feelings.

It is easy for Air dominant types to ignore their emotions. They can deny and rationalise any emotional issue that arises in their lives rather than feel them or confront them. There is nothing more powerful than a good argument to avoid real life conflicts, whether they are external or internal. However, once they have extended beyond their comfort zone emotionally and their life is falling apart, they will gladly attend counseling. The secret is to then engage them in a therapeutic aproach that is partly Air / intellectual and partly emotional. They really do want to understand their emotions but they can't do it by themselves.

An Air dominance is when the Luminaries (Sun and Moon) are in Air Signs (Gemini, Libra and Aquarius) and Houses (3rd, 7th and 11th). The Air Planets are: Mercury (rules both Gemini, active, and Virgo, passive), Venus (rules both Libra, active, and Taurus, passive) and Uranus which rules Aquarius. Even though Mercury also rules Virgo, and Venus also rules Taurus, both are Earth Signs, so they can double as Air Planets as well as Earth Planets. Mercury is most often considered an active Air Planet while Venus is more a passive Air Planet. Uranus is wholly Air and extremely strong in Air Signs and Houses.

A dominance in Air is increased when the Luminaries are also conjunct these Air Planets (Mercury, Venus and Uranus) and if they reside in any of the Air Signs. If there is a Stellium in an Air House such as the 3rd, 7th or 11th Houses then this amplifies the Air traits. Don't forget that an Air Signature also shows an Air dominance in the chart.

Air strengths include the ability to plan ahead and to fully review past history to predict the future. The Air Element dominates our accounting and legal fields; it is their mind that sets them apart from the other Elements. They can think around any problem and intuitively solve them without knowing how they did it. They also enter our homes through radio, TV and the social media - people with a strong Air Element are everywhere in our society. Computers, IT and social media are dominated by Air types, without them, our society would be totally lost.

The Air types will always trend towards communication and information, intellectual insight makes them feel most comfortable. They seek order through knowledge, objectivity and predictable explanations. They seek intellectual independence that helps make their life meaningful. They also turn up as the academic and sceptic who find security in intellectual pursuits rather than in emotional experiences.

They will often escape into fantasy, mystical and magical explanations or omens, to help make their life more predictable and to sooth the insecurities of those confusing, watery and inexplicable emotions.

A dominance in Air Signs shows us that the native may spend most of their time living inside their heads. They use this to defend against confusion, ambivalence and restricted freedom of expression. People with strong Air charts may also have problems keeping their feet on the ground.

An Air Sign's first line of defense is to reject any passionate explanation. Then they can engage their powerful rational conscious mind to counter any argument you may present. They need to be intellectually free, especially the Uranian / Aquarian types, to make their own choices and decisions. They also need to be able to escape into fantasy when emotional ambivalence gets out of hand.

It is important to remember that an Air 'emphasis' means for example that Uranus conjunct the Ascendant is mostly Air, even if the Ascendant is in a Water or Fire Sign; Moon conjunct Uranus is more Air than Water due to the stronger Outer Planet, etc. Learning to become an astrologer involves these simple strategies in finding Elementary dominance in people's charts.

Health-wise, we sometimes see problems with the senses, the eyes and ears, though this is quite rare. There may also be problems with touch, which brings the neurological disorders into the health picture. Such problems we might consider as communication difficulties like Asperger's and perhaps Parkinson's, though we really need much more research to have any confidence of this. So please don't rush out to your doctor for a diagnosis, this is still very theoretical.

Interestingly enough, although traditionally Air Planets, Signs and Houses link towards physical health problems, it is the mind I give the most attention, while I don't immediately notice physical ailments. For instance Air is involved in attentional and concentration problems seen in ADD and ADHD (Attention Deficit Disorder, Attention Deficit Hyperactive Disorder), nervousness, worry and stressed minds. One keyword stands out for Air dominance and it is 'worry'.

If there is an emphasis on Gemini (communication), we would expect issues with Mercury because Mercury Rules Gemini. Sometimes it is the hands and fingers, the sense of touch, there could be issues with arthritis, but it can also signal migraines and headaches, excessive worrying and perhaps some eye strain from lack of sleep (brought about by stress and worry).

Aquarius is also involved with the above issues but perhaps we would see a little more leaning towards detachment, difficulty connecting with others. We would look for ADD, neurological problems and the whole nervous system with a strong Aquarius or Uranus in the chart. I will often find Moon conjunct Uranus in clients presenting with worry and stress issues, disturbed sleep and relationship problems, especially at work.

Libra is particularly susceptible to confusion and ambiguity, unable to make up their mind and then they quickly lose focus and direction. They often have enormous problems in relationships where they compromise their freedom giving it all away to keep the peace. They will often be taken advantage of when they try to maintain harmony in their lives this way.

Their Air issue is their difficulty in managing confrontation. They strive to keep emotionally stable. If there is conflict in their relationships, they will compromise themselves to avoid any emotional distress. This can contribute to developing anxiety problems. In Air dominance, we see many relationship problems and emotional issues. Too much stress on the nervous system may possibly lead to neurological issues. Air involves the communication centres of the brain and as such may contribute to communication issues which can also manifest as headaches. Air dominance also suggests narcissistic traits and mental health issues in adults. In summary: an Air dominance in the chart can indicate concentration difficulties, denial of emotional problems, relationship issues, worry, disturbed sleep and possibly neurological difficulties.

Chart: Katie - *Air Planets and the Stellium in her 11th House (Air) - she has Mars, Saturn in Gemini in the 3rd House, adding to the Air emphasis with Gemini on the cusp of its own House; Pluto and Uranus in Libra in the 7th House also a double up on Air; Venus, Mercury and Jupiter in Aquarius in the 11th House add to Air. Is it any wonder that this lady has confused thoughts and excess worry?*

As she developed a greater understanding of herself and was able to talk through her problems over several years of therapy, and it did take years in therapy for her to process her life, she grew into an incredibly powerful lady. When she found out her husband was regularly meeting with prostitutes, she was able to remove herself mentally from the problem, work through it, by herself and in counseling, then come back to her husband with what she wanted. This she presented to her husband and they now have the fulfilling marriage (and sex life) they had both wanted. It was definitely not easy, but this lady had grown beyond what I have seen in many people in similar situations.

Air has its good points beyond worry. The detachment and logic of her Aquarian Stellium certainly played a huge part in her decisions, actions and final success through this crisis.

Katie

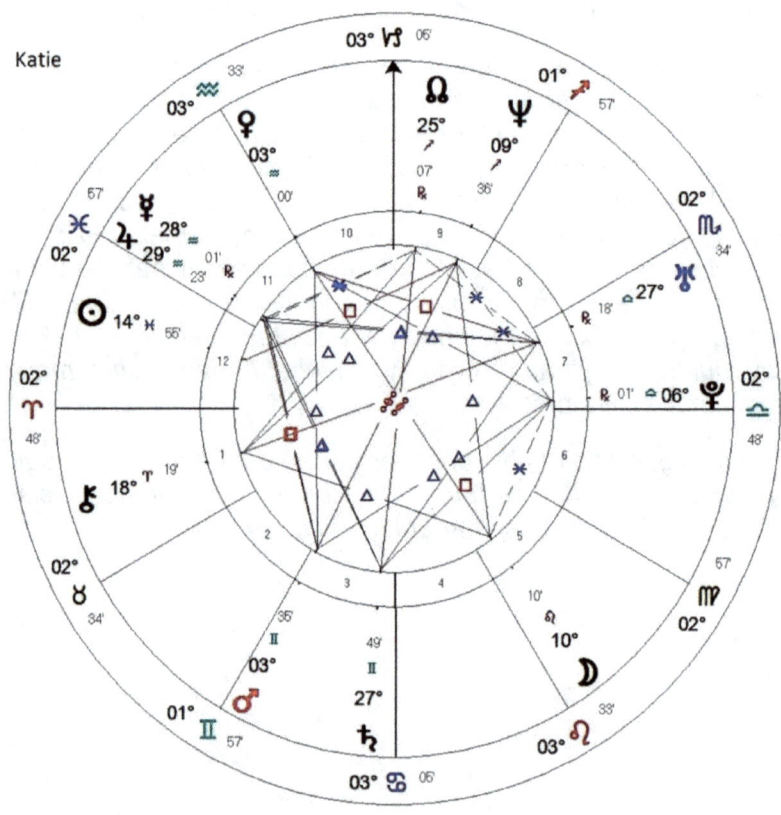

Magical Thinking of Air types - this reminds me of my good friend, Al. He once told me how he was invited to attend a workshop on how to manifest health goals into reality. The workshop leader taught the group how to meditate and to hold an image of their fully healed body in their mind, to then activate and manifest it in reality. To finalise the workshop he led the participants in a special meditation to project this activated and healed manifestation into their body to produce a total health transformation.

At the end of the meditation Al said that slowly, one by one, the participants opened their eyes to find their aged and unwell bodies transformed. As he looked around the group he watched as one by one they began to blink awake, but instead of joyfulness these faces slowly showed confusion and consternation.

My friend Al had severe arthritis since birth so he moved his hands and arms to see if his goal of freedom from pain and arthritis had truly manifested. He looked across at the others and they too were testing their bodies for this promised transformation. Al couldn't hold back any longer, *"Hey, mate. I don't feel any bloody different! I still have the same damn pain that I walked in here with 4 hours ago."*

Each participant nodded their head in agreement, nothing had changed. Al winked and said to me, *"That bloke had a clear-cut case of misplaced 'magical thinking'."* Al wasn't an astrologer but he had mastered the art of tarot better than anyone I knew. I am sure that he had tried every new-age therapy on the planet by this time. A very watery Piscean, he was looking for more than head-in-the-clouds magical promises.

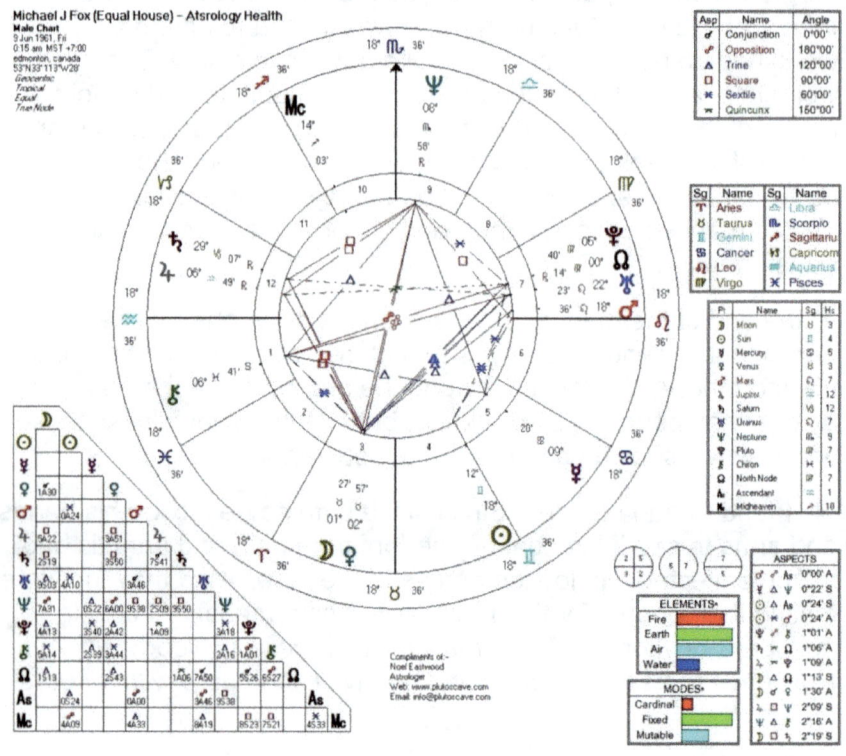

Chart: Michael J Fox - *Air dominance with Aquarius Ascendant, Stellium in the 7th House, Moon conjunct Venus in the 3rd House, Sun in Gemini - all amplify the Element Air. This is a strong Air chart, though the Earth Element is also indicated in the Element Grid through Taurus Moon, Venus, Capricorn Saturn and Virgoan Pluto with North Node. Always look at the House placements of Stelliums, Luminaries and Inner Planets. This is a very good reason why you should NEVER rely on the computer chart, always check for yourself.*

The 7th House is an Air House. It is very important to remember this when considering Elemental strength. A Stellium of four Planets in an Air House highlights the elemental characteristics of that House. Virgo is ruled by Mercury, which is another Air factor, so you also need to consider planetary Rulerships.

Lesson 2

Noel: *This lesson is about Air, and it is quite important when learning about mental health and astrology. The other Elements are most obviously physical but Air isn't, it is very hard to separate Air from personality traits such as those associated with denial and narcissism. Some key words are: intellect, of course, conscious mind and denial, dissociation. What are your thoughts on denial and dissociation? Not astrologically but as personality issues?*

Student: I've certainly witnessed both in Air people.

N - What could it mean if I said that someone was 'in denial'?

S - That there's something they're feeling or something going on that makes them uncomfortable and they pretend it's not there.

N - Perfect. A simple defence for emotional issues when you don't want others to know that you feel confused or distracted. If we go back to last week's lesson which introduced elemental defences and traits, we see that the Air defence is very effective as denial. Dissociation is much the same. Only this time they space out, become confused and can't concentrate. As a defence, this is quite effective too. They can avoid getting in touch with painful feelings.

Health issues would then relate to the conscious and unconscious mind and the senses. Mercury, Uranus and Venus are the Planets, as we know, and the Signs are Gemini, Libra and Aquarius... and the Houses 3, 7 & 11. We could go through their individual health issues, but that is too specific for us at the moment. What we seek to do here with the Elements is to lay a foundation. Earth foundations are power plays and retention / withholding, Air foundations are denial and dissociation.

Before we move on to the charts we'll look at ways we deny and dissociate. Can you give me an example of 'denial', from the notes or life is fine.

S - An alcoholic who won't face the fact that he/she is an alcoholic. Says, "I just drink socially."

N - So, what we would look for in the chart to see if this person is airy or may indulge in denial, is an emphasis on Air: Air Planets on the Angles, especially 1st and 10th, Planets in the 3rd 7th and 11th Houses, an emphasis on the Signs Gemini, Libra and

Aquarius. And we seek an emphasis only, not specifics yet, just a trend towards Air. For example an emphasis on Gemini would show an inclination towards talking over the top of you when you get too close to touchy subjects. An Aquarius type may try Magical Thinking. They say that the Martians will save us if only we pray enough at midnight. Magical Thinking is seen in our common superstitions and the new age has its own swath of superstitions while Libra may deny relationship problems. Now we begin to get a little more specific. When there is too much emphasis on Air, the nervous system overloads. This could be sensory nerves, or motor nerves or autonomic nerves. To prove this theory, we would need to look for a correlation in neurological disorders such as Parkinson's, Tourette Syndrome, Asperger's, Autism, ADD and ADHD, Bipolar Disorder, Schizophrenia, Obsessive Compulsive Disorder, Multiple Sclerosis... maybe? But I fear that this is beyond just an Air dominance and certainly needs far more research before we would draw any conclusions. It includes a hyperactive or very active mind, racing thoughts, difficulty sleeping because of thinking too much.

S - Blindness or hearing loss including selective blindness and hearing?

N – *Yes, that could be a form of denial too, headaches may also be used as a form of denial, though we may need more research on this. When stressed we can develop migraines. An example would be when someone has to go out somewhere that they don't want to go to: it can manifest as a migraine.*

Let's look at **Michael J Fox's chart.** *If our thesis is somewhere close to what I said it could be: that an emphasis on Air Signs and Houses and Planets makes for a disorder involving nerves and the mind; then Michael has some interesting features. You will note that I have used the Equal House System because the Placidus and Koch Systems both produce huge imbalances in the House sizes.*

S- I was wondering about that. Makes sense though.

N - *Yes some astrologers use Equal House system all the time. I only use it for charts with extremely large Houses which tend to make the chart quite useless for my work. Michael has an Air Ascendant, it is Aquarius which is very neurological. It rules the nervous system and may be implicated in nervous disorders. I would say that Aquarius is also related to kundalini as well. The* electrical system is the nervous system. Chiron is in the 1st House, and thus of primary importance. Chiron is the Fundamental Wound that Liz Greene talks about in her book, "Boundaries and Barriers'. Important even though Chiron is in Water; Moon and Venus are in the 3rd. Here we see an emphasis on the 3rd House of the conscious mind; Sun is in the Air Sign of Gemini. There is a powerful 7th House Stellium and Jupiter is also in Air. There are some strong indicators that Michael is more Air than any other the other Elements, would you agree?

S - Quite.

N - We would also say that he displayed elements of ADHD - the impulsive and hyperactive type, in his TV and movie performances. And now he has Parkinson's Disease, which he initially denied and finally came to terms with. Did you know that Air is also heavily implicated in alcoholism?

S - No, I thought we looked for Neptune and Pisces for addiction.

N - If we looked at addiction charts we would see a predominance of Air and then Fire. Water is a little different with depression and loss / grief but not so strong for alcoholism.

S - I was thinking about Fire as well in terms of running away from painful emotions. Fox actually was drinking for a while but he came out of it.

N - Fire is certainly 'running' but not so much on the denial bit. Yes Michael was drinking pretty heavily too. Alcoholism is definitely an Air defence. Drinking to stop those racing thoughts and to get some sleep. We certainly need another fifty charts of people with Parkinson's to really prove our theory. Before we move on. Any comments or questions about Fox?

S - I also think the Mars-Uranus Opposition to the Aquarian Ascendant is bound to be stressful on the nervous system. Mars-Uranus is pretty stressful by itself.

N - Yes and as the ruler of the Ascendant, Uranus is powerful and may easily contribute to his health problems.

*Chart: **Mariah** - note the Libra Stellium in the earthy 6th House, Taurus Ascendant, both Taurus and Libra are ruled by Venus. Chiron is the Planet of High Degree at the very top of the chart so her fundamental wound involves striving for her goals. Moon in Scorpio conjunct Jupiter and Moon sits on her 7th House cusps of love and relationships.*

*By the way we can go back to Michael and his chart at any time in the course as we look at more things like Uranus and Mars Conjunctions, etc. So, **Mariah**. What do you see in her chart?*

Mariah

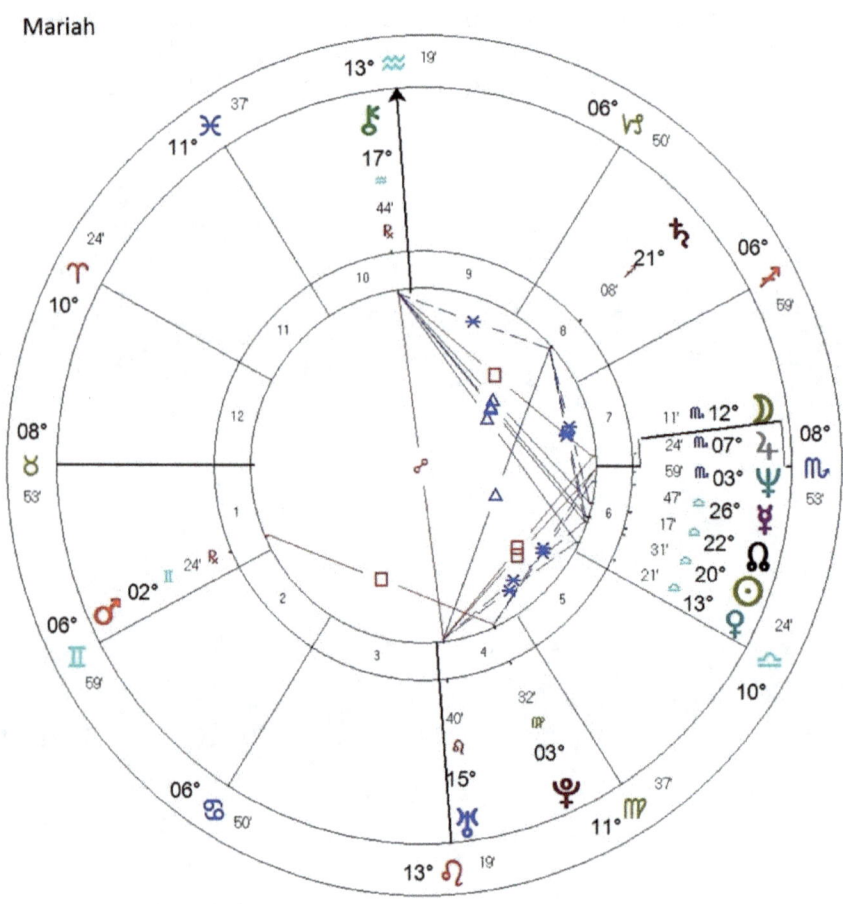

S - Libra Stellium including the Sun but also that Gemini Mars is lonesome in the east hemisphere. Also it is the only Planet in a personal Sign (Aries through Cancer), squared by Pluto and quincunxed by Neptune (if you're into quincunxes). Mars is also the (traditional) dispositor of her Scorpio Moon which is the focal point of a Fixed T-Square with Uranus and Chiron. Chiron in Aquarius on the MC (ouch). Mars also rules the 12th House.

N - Excellent. We see an emphasis on Mars in the 1st and an airy Libra Stellium in the 6th House which doubles as an earthy 6th House Stellium. Chiron is also in Air on the MC and most importantly Moon in Scorpio on the 7th conjunct Jupiter. T-Square with Uranus opposite Chiron Square Moon with focus on the Moon. A very intense and focused chart and also very angry and frustrated. There is an emphasis on Air especially related to Libra and the Scorpio Moon in the 7th House. There is a loaded 6th House(Earth) which certainly emphasises her physical symptoms of constipation, intestinal and renal. But it is the Air Element that tends to trigger her health issues. Straight away we see denial. Which area of her life does she live in denial of?

S - The Scorpio 7th House I suppose.

N - Yes exactly. With 7 points in Air / Libra there must be denial of her 7th House (Libran) issues - relationships. Librans seem to have lots of relationship problems. Mariah was married to an alcoholic husband who bashed her for most of their years together. The key word for Libra is 'compromise' so she compromised her safety for the needs of her husband and children. She said that she loved the sex. He was a mad sex machine but she had never had an orgasm with him. I hope this isn't too rude.

S - That is sad.

N – It sure it. I couldn't quite work that one out until I saw her strong Libra chart and realised that her denial was so very strong. Libra needs harmony, affection and to feel attractive. This made her blind to the reality of what was happening in her marriage. Astrology really helps a therapist understand issues that are not very clear. The Libra keyword is 'compromise' by my understanding.

S - Note also that Venus is her final dispositor: 'Peace at all Cost'.

N - Good on you for noticing that, I didn't. Her health would involve Libran issues which we get to later but her denial led to many years of abuse until at last she left him. He continues his abuse in other ways. Oh yeah I almost forgot, she has mental health issues and although she says that she hates men she still gets into every conceivable relationship with all sorts of nasty men. She may have suffered Bipolar Disorder but what we do see is this emphasis on Air. The good news is that after four years of on and off therapy, she is getting her life in order. She is so much better that she no longer exhibits any bipolar symptoms. An incredible woman.

Her kids experienced all sorts of problems, too. They witnessed the abuse and domestic violence at home. School authority figures can often trigger these issues. They lashed out as though school was their father. But as she got better so did they.

S - I always get nervous when I see Neptune in contact with either Mars or Saturn.

N - Good point. We should look at this later when we do the Water defence. Too much Air can lead to issues with relationships which is ruled by Libra, an Air Sign and the Airy 7th House. Venus is a major player here as the ruler of that Libra Stellium. She is both Earth (ruler of Taurus) and Air so we need to keep an eye on her. Any comments or questions?

S - It seems like she projects that Mars, no?

N - Oh yes, she sure does. She is very angry at men. She admits that she has incredibly violent tantrums in her relationships.

S - I've found that Chiron in hard aspect with the Sun or Moon needs years of therapy to overcome.

N - Very true. Let's look at her Mars. In the 1st House, so it really demands expression. Anything in the 1st needs expression and Aries, his Sign, is on the 12th cusp, which indicates her fears. She is afraid of her Mars in many ways. It can represent anger and violence. Mars is poorly aspected, as you said. We certainly know she was part of the domestic violence in her marriage. Both victim and perpetrator. She admitted that she initiated many of the arguments and assaults as did her ex-husband. Then Chiron. He is very much the one in need of therapy, too. Sitting at the top of the chart and conjunct the MC, Chiron is one of the focal Planets in the chart. Chiron holds sway over her drive, ambitions, etc. It suggests many years of therapy.

S - Just to add that the Chiron-Uranus Opposition is on the cusps of the parental Houses. Her own parents must've been a howl.

N - *Yes that is a great observation. She hates them and her ex-husbands parents, as well.*

S - She needs to vent to overcome her Venus-Libra thing.

N - *I forgot to add that there was sexual abuse as a child by a male neighbour that we worked on in therapy. She tells me that she gets into sexual relationships quite easily. Her 1st House Mars needs sexual expression just as much as other means of physical expression. The good news is that she is a hundred times better than when she began therapy and she loves astrology and doing my courses. Catch you next week.*

Chapter 3

Fire Dominance in Health

A Fire dominant person feels the need to defend against insignificance, boredom, inertia, personal meaninglessness, impotence, criticism, vulnerability, humiliation and the feeling of being totally ignored and worthless. They seek to compete with others for attention, seeks to be perceived as special - they leantowards narcissism, rivalry, jealousy and envy.

Liz Greene and Howard Sasportas, in their book *The Development of the Personality*, describe the Fire Element as aligning with the Greek myth of King Oedipus. Dr Sigmund Freud proposed that the 'Oedipus Complex' was a psychological complex defending someone against overwhelming humiliation, guilt, insignificance and inertia. The native therefore competes in one-upmanship, seeking attention, and sometimes this involves bullying and/or fighting for recognition. These driven, self-seeking behaviours provide meaning and fulfilment in their lives and ably demonstrate many of the traits seen in a Fire dominant astrological profile.

The myth is about King Oedipus of ancient Greece, who unknowingly killed his father and married his mother. According to psychodynamic theory, this is seen as a male child seeking to kill or conquer his father so that he can have his mother all to himself.

Greene and Sasportas echo Dr's Jung and Freud's extensive and ground breaking works. The theory suggests that the mother is the boy's first love and his father now becomes an obstacle that stands between the boy and his mother. The child seeks to manoeuvre and gain power by colluding with the mother to remove the father (and often the mother initiates this manoeuvre). We see this in dyads whereby mother and child ally against the father. Once the father is defeated, he becomes 'castrated', impotent and powerless in the family dynamic.

I would add that this behaviour occurs not just with mothers and sons but also with mothers and daughters or fathers with sons and daughters. This is not pure psychodynamic theory, of course. But collusion and dyads, power plays, occur between all family members at one time or another. Family dynamics is another topic altogether and a fascinating field of study.

Sometimes it is the child who loses and becomes 'castrated' himself. Castration was Freud's way of describing a loss of power, impotence. Whoever loses the battle to gain the mother is overpowered and defeated. I will sometimes see this in my practice with men whose children have been turned against them by their mother, often after a divorce. It is not limited to sons. It can also happen with daughters, as well.

Sometimes a son dominates their overly needy mother who lacks self-esteem or self-worth, who cannot get love and affection in other ways. This dominating, narcissistic son is reasonably common in single male-child families or a single mother with an only child, usually a son. In these dysfunctional families, the mother will actively collude with the son to 'castrate' or disempower the father.

Where there is no father living at home an example would be: a Fire dominant son controling his Water dominant mother who choses to interpret his control and bullying as affection. I am sure this happens in female only child families as well, where the girl child plots with the father to castrate the mother. I have rarely encountered this phenomenon in my practice though. I think the dominant position of the mother as the primary caregiver during infancy is a key factor in these Fire complexes.

Once having castrated the father (or mother or siblings), the Fire dominant child can go on to develop overly strong narcissistic, bullying traits. This may present in seeking to gain dominion and power over others in later years.

One of the manifestations of the Fire complex can be seen in sibling rivalry. The children form dyads and triads, ganging up into pairs and triplets to defeat a common foe, be that another sibling, step sibling or step parent. I recommend R.D. Laing's *The Divided Self* for further reading on this topic.

On a positive note, Fire strengths include the ability to start something new where no opportunities existed even moments before. Every day is an adventure to people with Fire dominant traits. They are seen shining in the sports fields, in the cinema, at parties and in leadership: they love the limelight. Want someone to head up an expedition or to give the keynote address at your next presentation? There is no one more delighted than an inspired Fire Sign.

Without Fire people, we wouldn't have brave heroes to worship in sports, war or those fascinating personalities who brave the elements in our movies, books and adventure magazines. Fire dominance is highlighted by human creativity and inspiration like a burning brightness that draws us to their flame. We can't avoid being drawn to an inspired role or a passionate romance in a play - Fire attracts but it also burns if mishandled.

Fire dominance is found when there is a focus on Fire Signs (Aries, Leo and Sagittarius); Fire Houses (1st, 5th and 9th) and the Fire Planets (Sun, Mars and Jupiter). Fire is emphasised when Mars and Jupiter are strongly placed in the chart such as in the 1st, 5th and 9th or Fire Houses; or in the Angluar Houses\ (1st, 4th, 7th, 10th). It is seen with the Luminaries (Moon and Sun) in a Fire Sign or House and particularly when they are conjunct Mars or Jupiter. Other indicators include a Fire Ascendant or a Fire Signature. Also look for a Stellium (a group of 4 or more Planets) in a Fire Sign or House.

Please note: Not all Fire dominant people 'castrate' their father to dominate the mother. That was just one of many directions that psychotherapy developed back in the early 20th century. Drawing upon Greek mythology was their way to help understand the dynamics that they were encountering in depth analysis. It is best to think of it as someone who seeks to be the centre of attention, exhibits narcissistic behaviour patterns, who is often quite selfish and bullying.

Don't forget the Fire dominant person's positive characteristics either. These are spectacular qualities that many of us admire and wish to emulate.

What do the Fire Signs want most? They want to be noticed. They are the children, the attention-seekers of the zodiac. They burn with enthusiasm and consume large amounts of energy creating and then conquering their world.

Health problems that can develop for Fire Signs include fevers, inflammation, congested energy leading to chronic pain, impatience, irritability, various substance and physical addictions, hypertension, hyperactivity, strong libido and overactive kidney and adrenal glands.

Too much Fire in a chart can lead to high temperatures, high blood pressure, heart problems, liver and kidney problems and excessive sweating. They need to drink a lot of water. Playing physically in water is one great way for them to calm down and cool off.

The Fire Planet, Jupiter, seeks an outlet for his enthusiasm through addictions; Sun seeks praise for his good works and indulgences; while Mars seeks physical challenges to accomplish and conquer. Each want to experience all that life has to offer—and this requires a lot of energy.

Rather than leaping at every opportunity, they need a 'confidence buffer', someone who helps guide them, nurture them, help them make good choices. Often a 'broken' Fire Sign will struggle to recover their confidence when they have a set-back. An illness has the potential to stifle their will to go on and depression is their greatest enemy.

Fire Signs can also sap the life-force from those around them when they are ill. Don't forget that illness has its own rewards. If you get a lot of attention by being sick, then you might wish to stay sick and get more attention.

Fire Signs control overtly. They shout, threaten and jump up and down. You are never left in any doubt as to what it is they want. They can be very noisy and loud when they don't get their way.

Some health problems we would consider are addictions of indulgence, food, drugs, alcoholism, narcissism, egocentricity and selfishness. The biggest problem, especially with Jupiter, is addictions, gambling, drugs, sex, parties and alcohol. Kidney and bladder problems can arise as they burn up a lot of fuel (energy) and tend to drink very little fresh water. They can also consume large amounts of coffee and alcohol.

In summary: health problems arise when there is an emphasis on Mars, Sun and Jupiter, Stelliums in the 1st, 5th and 9th Houses and Planets in the Fire Signs: Aries, Leo and Sagittarius and on the Angles.

Chart: Carlie - a Stellium in the Fire 9th House which consists of the Luminaries, Sun and Moon both conjunct Fire Jupiter, who is exalted, or emphasised in his own House. This little group of Planets is dynamite. Mars opposes both Luminaries creating friction and heat, irritability and a need to blame or verbally attack someone.

Note that although not all Fire Houses are emphasised, and Carlie's 1st and 5th Houses have no Planets, we still consider this a strong Fire chart. Earth is also strong with Capricorn Ascendant and Moon and Sun in Virgo. This demonstrates that in astrology we never rely on a single Planet, Sign, House or Element to be more than what it is. They all form part of the native's entire life. Many of Carlie's traits will include Earth qualities, but it is the Fire traits we discuss in the following lesson transcript.

Carlie

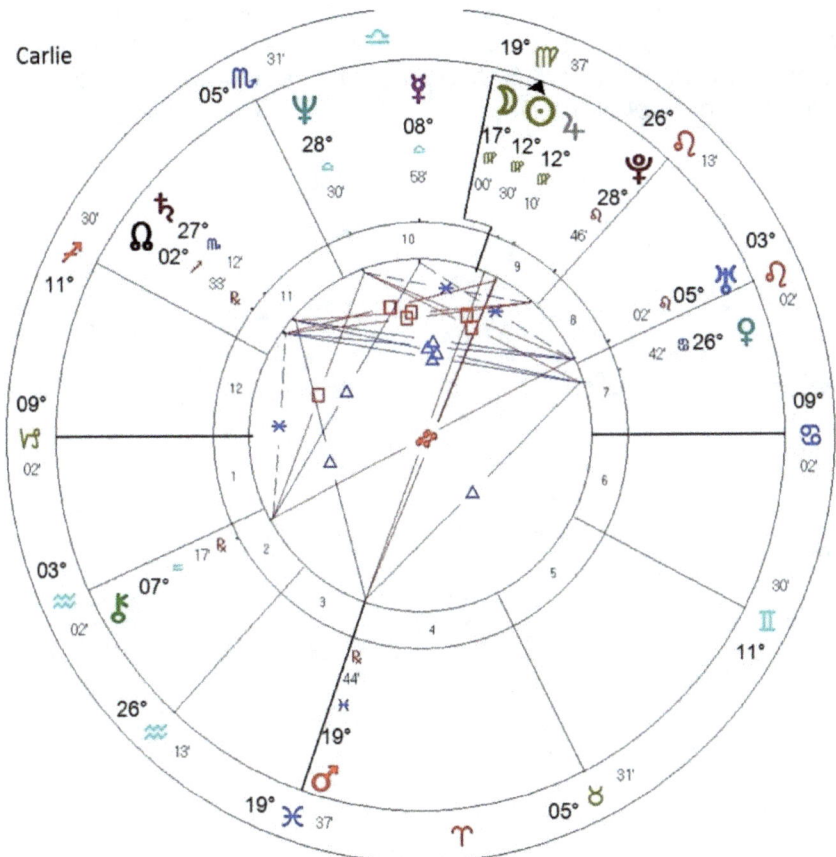

Chart: Judie - *note that this also has strong Earth and Air, it is the Fire dominance of Jupiter conjunct her Capricorn Ascendant and Mars applying to her 5th House cusp that seem to have taken complete control of her life.*

Judie

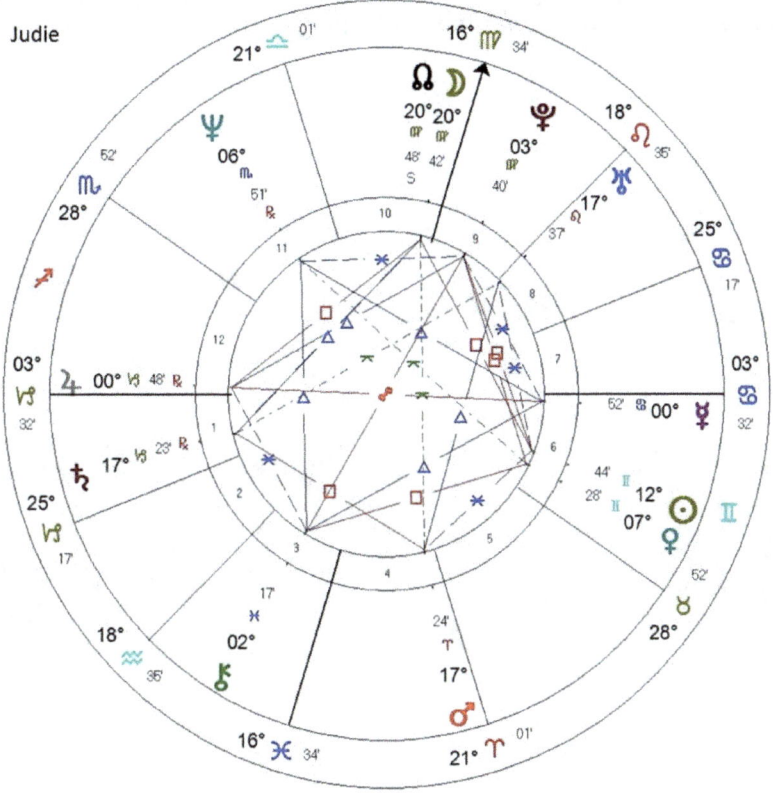

Chart: Gale - *Mars and Sun in Aries plus a Fire Signature are the key Fire points we discuss in Gale's lesson. This chart also contains strong Water dominance as well and is a good example of combining both Elements in a reading.*

Gale

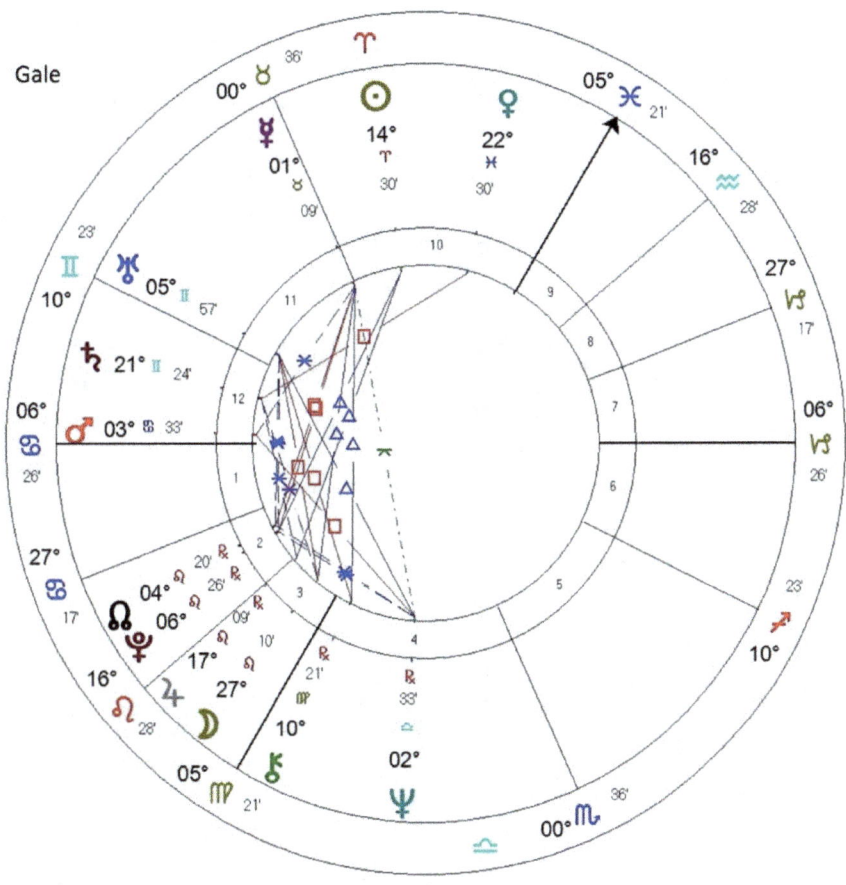

Chart: Baby Barbara - Fire dominance, *Aries Ascendant and both Luminaries in Leo in the 5th House* led to this little girl developing overheating problems and fever fits while teething.

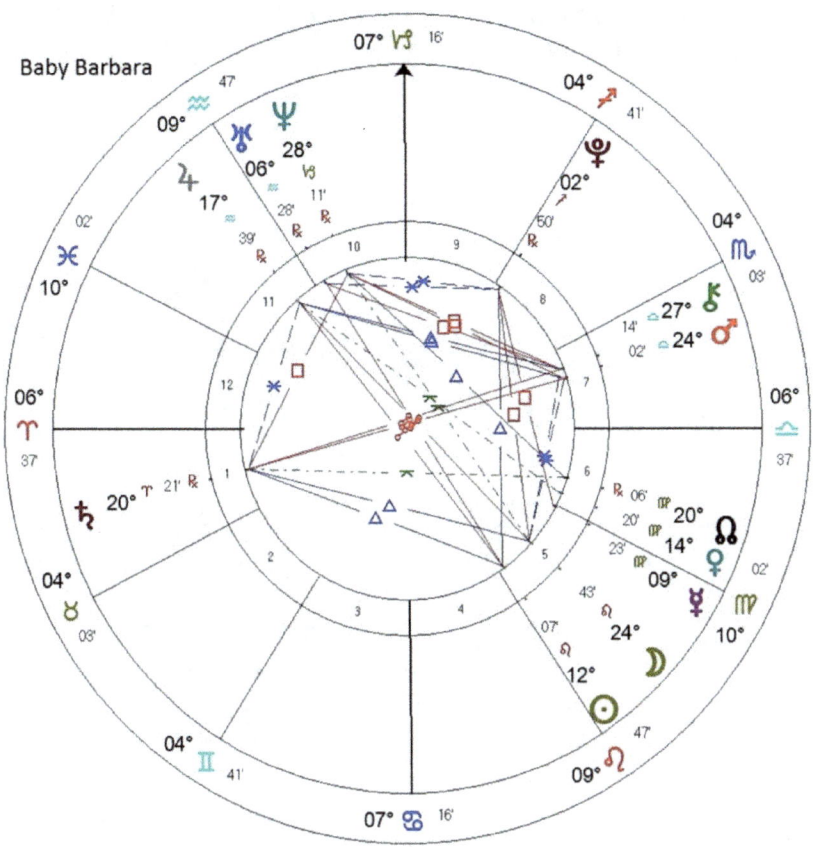

Chart: Martyn - *Sagittarius Ascendant conjunct Jupiter plus Sun in Aries and Mars / Mercury in the fiery 5th House contribute to Martyn's health issues.*

Martyn

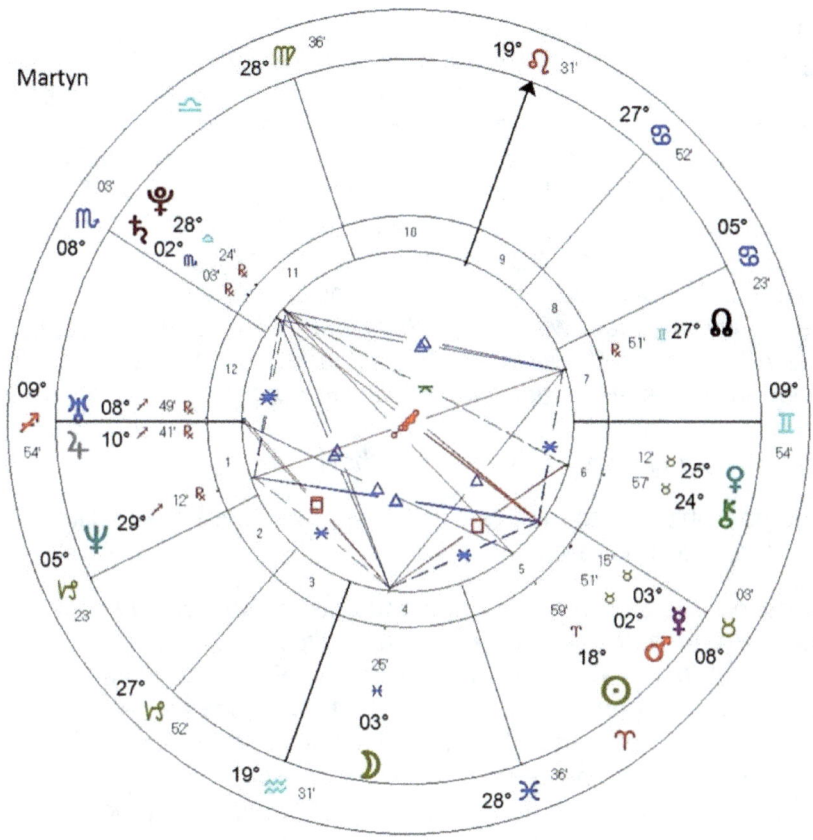

Lesson 3

Noel: *Ready for some Fire astrology? Fire is also very psychological, hyperactive and physical. It involves narcissistic traits. The best way to think of Fire is as the key to activity: energy. They just want more and more. More stimulation, adrenaline rush; they develop heat, fevers and high temperatures. Too much Fire leads to very childish behaviour. They can be egocentric, self-centred and narcissistic. If we look at excess Fire, we see these signs early in the child's behaviour. In infancy, they are poor sleepers, susceptible to fevers, high temperatures and of course hyperactivity. Mothers will say that their baby didn't even sleep in the womb. They start walking by 9 months, the usual is 12 months. Grandparents, relatives and friends start to put their brittle glassware up at least 3 feet into the air when the family comes for a visit. You must know a few kids like that?*

Student: Don't look at me I was an angel. I've heard of kids like that. Glad I don't have one.

N - I have three of them, two Aries and one Libran. They usually have scars on their heads from their many falls. As they grow, they do sort themselves out a bit. Generally, Fire people are quite bright, they are sharp, funny and generous. We look to the Fire Planets: Sun, Jupiter and Mars; and their Signs: Leo, Sagittarius and Aries. We do sometimes confuse Air qualities with Fire qualities in children. Both together are fascinating, smart, active, high achievers but in a small few they are susceptible to narcissistic behaviours, addictions, inability to wind down and even criminal behaviours given the right opportunities and experiences. We would of course seek to find Fire Signs on the Angles; Stelliums and Grand Trines are Fire patterns. Stelliums in the Fire Signs and in Houses 1, 5 and 9 emphasise Fire. Their health issues begin at birth with hyperactivity, temperatures and fevers. As they get older, this generally passes without any major problems. In early childhood they seek sweets, candy / lollies to keep their energy up. Then, as teenagers and young adults. they move to coffee, chocolate, sex, alcohol and drugs. A Fire dominant person loves physical energy and burns it up more than the other Elements. It is the beginning of their need to maintain high energy levels and they certainly feel good when on a high. That is why sugar helps even at an early age. In their teens they seek other stimulants. Then there is their outlandish and dangerous behaviour. This is the typical teenage rage period doing dangerous stunts for a dare, car races, jumping off bridges, drinking to excess. You know what I mean.

S - Not directly I was a good girl.

N - Of course you were and I bet you have some interesting stories to tell off-line. As they pass this adrenaline stage, they grow into driven, motivated and successful leaders and businessmen, sports heroes, teachers, etc. Most of our successful people have high levels of Fire and Air. If it is too over-bearing it might lead to criminal behaviours. Too much of a good thing is not so good. If there is an abundance of Fire and Air, we would consider Attention Deficit Hyperactive Disorder (ADHD); then as the environment deteriorates, we consider family dysfunction, peer pressure, criminal friends, opportunities to commit crimes, etc. Then there are the cases of over-abundance, not just dominance, of Fire and Air: psychopathy. They lack empathy, have no feelings, cold and uncaring, they lack an understanding of the pain they cause to others. These are the politicians, managers, CEO's, businessmen and women who bully their staff, rip off their shareholders, even religious leaders who control, abuse and bully their flock. **Note** *that 'psychopathy' is not a singularly Fire or Air trait. It is an unusual combination of the two Elements in very dominant placements that must first be triggered by environment and opportunity. This is not just a male thing either. Women are just as likely to exhibit these qualities and participate in these activities and traits as men. A good web site for researching this phenomenon is* www.crimelibrary.com *. Another site is* www.mayhem.com *You can check them out yourself, well worth looking at.*

All this self-centred rushing about builds up Fire in the body which of course requires plenty of water to keep the body cool, to evaporate, sweat, urinate, reduce the lactic acid build-up, etc. Excess Fire creates wastes which need to be removed. Those excess stimulants may damage organs such as the liver (Jupiter) and kidneys (partly Venus and Mars) and the heart which tries to keep it all running (Sun).

S - Excellent summary! And it explains a lot about certain people I know.

N - Thanks. This is still the basic foundations for the patterns we see in the chart.

S - I've had dealings with Fire people, mostly Leos.

N - *I always think of Homer Simpson as a Leo type. Now we look at **Carlie's chart** - alcoholic. Notice anything?*

S - I'm ready for you this time. I went through all the charts earlier today. Sun conjunct Jupiter in the 9th, Pluto also in the 9th, Jupiter rules the 12th House, Sun-Jupiter also conjunct Moon-MC, all opposed by Mars, partile conjunct the IC. Also Mars is in the only Transpersonal Sign. Leo is on the cusp of a loaded 9th House. Are you using Placidus or Koch?

N - *Koch. I nearly always do and especially for this subject. Bright student you are. You sure are doing well for a Friday night.*

S - That's all I've got.

N - *Yes we can immediately see that the 9th is loaded. Then we notice that Moon and Sun reside there, the two Luminaries, a very important 9th House to start with. We keep looking and notice that Leo is on its cusp and that Jupiter, the big magnifying glass, is conjunct them. Add to that Mars is opposing them. So, as you already told me, we have a loaded 9th. Now the 9th is also a Fire / Sagittarian House ruled by Jupiter. Can you please give me some key words we will use for the 9th and Jupiter and maybe the Leo influence.*

S - Enthusiasm, optimism, adventuresome, explorer, preacher, good-humoured, jokester. Her occupation? Don't tell me. There's that Capricorn rising and Virgo stuff. Could be some kind of professor, maybe a trial lawyer, or an athletic coach?

N - *Cold, something to do with the body, offices and planes.*

S - Not an Air traffic controller?

N - *Wow. Close, but not quite. She is a travel agent.*

S - Ohhhh duh.

N - *That's when she is not drinking herself sick.*

S - Right Question. You'd say the addiction Planet is Jupiter, not Neptune, right?

N - *Correct, yes, she had traveled overseas heaps, and had lots of affairs. Not that this is necessarily part of the 9th but it is of Jupiter. She was also a top model, a very beautiful lady.*

S - OK, that makes it more interesting.

N - We will get to Neptune next week. I told you this was a slightly different approach to the traditional one, so please hang in there. The sex bit is Jupiter's abundance and irresponsible behaviours. He tends to ignore social boundaries and behavioural rules, a bit like Neptune can do. However, the Capricorn Ascendant and Virgo Sun / Moon would of course temper this a bit, which it does. Only two affairs at the one time, very Jupiterian, and Neptune, who can help erase boundaries and limitations.

S - Sounds awfully dull to me.

N - Health problems of course relate to mental health. Not delusional or anything like that but rather erratic mood swings and depression which is probably the Earth thing happening. Liver problems from excess alcohol, overweight, disturbed sleep. She came for counseling for her depression but we soon discovered that her alcoholism was important and that perhaps the depression was driving her alcohol and food addiction. She wrote a romance novel sitting at home depressed and drinking. She sadly became very overweight. She was once a model, stunningly beautiful. She was such a generous and caring person. She had so much going for her but sometimes the bottle wins over counseling. Any comments on Carlie?

S - Just about the romance novel thing and depression. She has a Venus-Neptune Square and Venus-Saturn Trine. Romantic dreams that never come true?

N - There is more on this in the Water lesson next week but that was a really insightful astrological observation. Love and betrayal, Neptune Square Venus - always the mistress never the bride. But she should be able to stay in relationships despite this with a Venus Trine Saturn and a strong Capricorn - but yes that Square can be damaging.

S - A serious romantic.

N - Writing a novel has a lot to do with the 9th House and Jupiter, verbosity, doesn't need Mercury to write. Fire is good at romance, in fact the most romantic types are Fire Signs because they have a burning passion, particularly if there is Water in the mix. Romance and the Four Elements: - **Air:** think about it. **Water:** dream about it and get depressed with it. **Earth:** argue over it while **Fire** will live it.

Next chart: **Judie,** do you see Jupiter lurking on the Ascendant?

S - Jupiter ruling 12th on her Ascendant, yes.

N - And Air Gemini Sun and Venus in the 6th, Saturn in the 1st House. We can safely say that she is susceptible to mood swings too. Depression with Saturn and elation with Jupiter. Then add Air Gemini for extra moodiness and excessive thinking. The Moon on the MC can make her moods more pronounced.

S - Mars trine Uranus, square Saturn.

N - Yes, please tell me what that means?

S - Mars-Uranus is great willfulness, edginess, suppressed, or rather inhibited by Saturn. There is also a Moon-Mercury mutual reception. The Moon squares the Sun and Mercury opposes Jupiter. Fire on cusp of 5th and 9th Houses.

N - Good. Judie is alcoholic, depressed, obsessive compulsive at times and she is as lazy as can be. A narcissistic user of other people with some classic negative Jupiter behaviours: addictive and irresponsible. Her long standing partner has just split with her too. She isn't one of my clients just someone I know of. She is mixed up and sometimes nasty. Health? Female organs and liver problems - of course. From memory, I think that she has had some miscarriages. This would contribute to her depression, drinking and mood swings as well.

Baby Barbara: *A very interesting case. Here we have emphasis on Leo and the 5th She was rushed to hospital with fever fits at about 2 years of age. With a quick check we see too much Fire. Aries Ascendant. She may develop hyperactivity later in her childhood. This can sometimes be seen with Air and Fire dominant in the chart. Look for Air and Fire on the 1st, 3rd, 5th, 7th, 9th and 11th House cusps. I suggested (and I am not a medical professional so don't take this as gospel) that the parents cut out cow's milk and any sugary drinks, give her lots of water to drink, keep her cool and give her lots of fresh raw fruit and other yin water foods, reduce yang, like wheat. Her immediate need was reduce Fire, can you see that?*

S - Heck yeah, amazing.

N - **Gale,** *kidney cancer, a lot of Fire, Aries especially.*

S - One second, occupations (if any) for the last three?

N - Judie, office work, receptionist, Baby Barbara, a baby, of course and Gale was an astrologer.

S - Hey!

N - Sadly she died some years ago, a very driven lady, too.

S - Aw.

N - Yeah. I became quite close to her and her family. We see some ADHD stuff here with lots of Fire, Leo and Mars, Aries Sun. Jupiter is implicated again with Moon. She must have been hard to live with at times and by all accounts she was. Again, we see water needs for such a driven high-powered Fire personality.

S - Ahem, I have a Moon-Jupiter Conjunction.

N - Where?

S - Scorpio.

N - Oops. Note to self, "must not put foot in mouth".

S - Ha ha.

N - OK, **Martyn**, drug addictions. Note Jupiter and Uranus, they make for a moderate ADHD profile. Actually, a nice kid. He works for his dad's timber business but goes out partying and gets stoned on weekends. Doesn't touch alcohol or dope but loves the fast stuff just like someone with Jupiter and Uranus conjunct his Sagittarius Ascendant would. Note also Sun in Aries in the 5th House: both are Fire.

S - I thought it was interesting that Martyn's family is in the timber business and he has all that Taurus in his chart.

N - Yeah? I didn't notice that.

S - This is a good way to learn about the Elements. I mean it would help if they were all taught this way including the associated pathologies.

N - Psychopathology is fascinating. When astrology is used in conjunction with psychology, so much more comes out for therapists to work with. At the moment my research is looking at Elements and psychopathology but it might take years to finish. Research takes so much time.

S - Research is like that

N - I will post next lesson and transcripts. If you have any questions on this lesson please just email me. Good night

Chapter 4

Water Dominance in Health

Water dominance defends against the emotions of abandonment, betrayal, neglect, rejection and loneliness by attaching to others and / or to love objects.

Freud explained that our first reflex at birth is to suckle at our mother's breast, our first love object is our mother. Feelings of warmth, attachment, belonging, love, joy, nurturing, satisfaction and fulfilment come from this initial experience. When the child is weaned and the breast is withdrawn, it can sometimes set off a need for a substitute breast such as a toy, food, a dummy / pacifier, thumb sucking, a nanny, etc. These substitutes displace the real breast.

If the infant's emotional (Water) needs are not met, they can become fixated at the Water stage of development. They will seek substitutes: other people or objects and commonly it is food and romance novels.

The oral reflex is a natural phenomenon. Suckling is a powerful experience for the newborn. It's much like our first encounter with a stranger. Our first impression will always last the longest. Imagine that the breast is withdrawn before the child is fulfilled and satisfied. A yearning begins, a yearning that can manifest as a defence.

A Water defence is seen when a native experiences abandonment or betrayal by a loved one. When their relationship breaks up they feel loss and their grief is greater than would normally be expected. I see abandonment issues every day in my practice. It provides therapists with a lot of their work.

Water strengths include the ability to empathise with others, to feel compassion and to engage fully in nurturing. Healers of all kinds have a strong Water Element. We also find them in the creative arts: writers, media professionals, visual artists and musicians. They expand our world through their vision.

Astrologers find Water dominance when the Sun, or more commonly the Moon, is in a Water Sign, a Water House or in poor aspect with the Outer Planets: Neptune, Chiron and Pluto. To find Water defence in the chart we need to look for a poorly aspected Moon. Often this is not in a Water Sign but in Conjunction with an

Outer Planet in the 4th, 8th or 12th House. Sometimes this can be seen in the 7th House, if there is a Water dominance in that House.

In terms of physical health, a fear of abandonment can lead to depression and the need to run into one's cave to self-nurture - or to run to someone: the serial romancer always in love with someone. Water Signs, Cancer, Scorpio and Pisces, and the Planets Moon, Pluto and Neptune all tend to have a tender or sensitive physical body. They can suffer rejection worse than Fire types, they tend to internalise and convert emotional pain into physical symptoms.

Moon or Lunar types, need to be needed and if not they can feel ignored, disconnected and thus abandoned. To prevent this from happening they manipulate and blackmail those around them to stay needed. Pluto controls through emotional blackmail, too. Pluto types become dependent on their partners for emotional security. It can be very difficult to reject these Plutonians because their partner feels so very flattered to be so needed and desired. However, the emotional roller-coaster of jealousy and control can become too much.

Neptune escapes into fantasy land, dissociating to somewhere else when they feel abandoned. They don't blackmail, but they do control through illness and by abandoning their own physical needs - eating, drinking and personal care. Neptunians can manifest emotional illnesses such as asthma and nervous disorders when they don't address their emotional needs. They convert their emotional pain into physical pain and they can show extreme sensitivity to any form of pain especially in their feet. They will use pain killers excessively if allowed.

Their other manifestations are psychological: depression and anxiety and even some forms of delusion. They adapt wonderfully to any situation but run the risk of losing themselves in the process.

In relationships, Water Signs need to be loved and will exist in all forms of abusive, violent domestic relationships just to experience affection. It is said, *"Women will swap sex for love, while men will swap love for sex."* Sometimes Water types become trapped seeking emotional attachment to avoid feeling abandoned.

Please don't think that men are the only perpetrators of domestic violence. Domestic violence comes in many forms, emotional abuse, manipulation and emotional neglect are common passive forms of domestic violence. Men tend to act out when hurt, they become physically and overtly violent and abusive, hitting and inflicting physical pain and injuries. Women on the other hand tend to become covertly abusive (secret, hidden), using emotional abuse and neglect, psychological abuse and injuries. I treat many men and women who are in violent domestic relationships and physical abuse is used just as much by women as by men.

There is ample evidence that women initiate domestic violence at the same rate as males. Abusive partners, no matter what gender, are still perpetrators of domestic violence. It is not limited to either gender.

A strong Water chart indicates the potential for the native to feel some form of abandonment and fear of betrayal. If Pluto or Mars are in Fire or Air and they are accompanied by a strongly placed Aries Moon, for example, it can suggest physical aggression. If you see abandonment in a chart, look also for overt or covert abuse in their relationships. This can be coming from them or directed at them.

Water types tend to control covertly, they use emotional and psychological manipulation. It is similar to Earth dominance control through the withholding and giving of affection. However, Water dominant types run things through their neediness, their victim behaviour, which makes others feel sorry for them.

Plutonic types withdraw into their cave when emotionally hurt or needy. They feel their partner withdraw, so they withdraw too. A Plutonic couple will dance backwards and forwards between their caves and the safe middle ground, often without even knowing it.

Charts: Anthony and Terri – natal

Anthony—*anger, relationships, binge drinking. Look at cusps, especially Pluto and Uranus conjunct the 12th House cusp, plus Sun and Chiron conjunct the 6th cusp.*

Terri—*fiery relationships (1st House Stellium), stomach and digestion (Virgo Stellium), stress (Moon in Gemini conjunct MC). Not much Water, but look at Pluto conjunct Sun and Ascendant, Moon conjunct MC. Controlling, emotionally abusive?*

Terri-top chart

Anthony-bottom chart

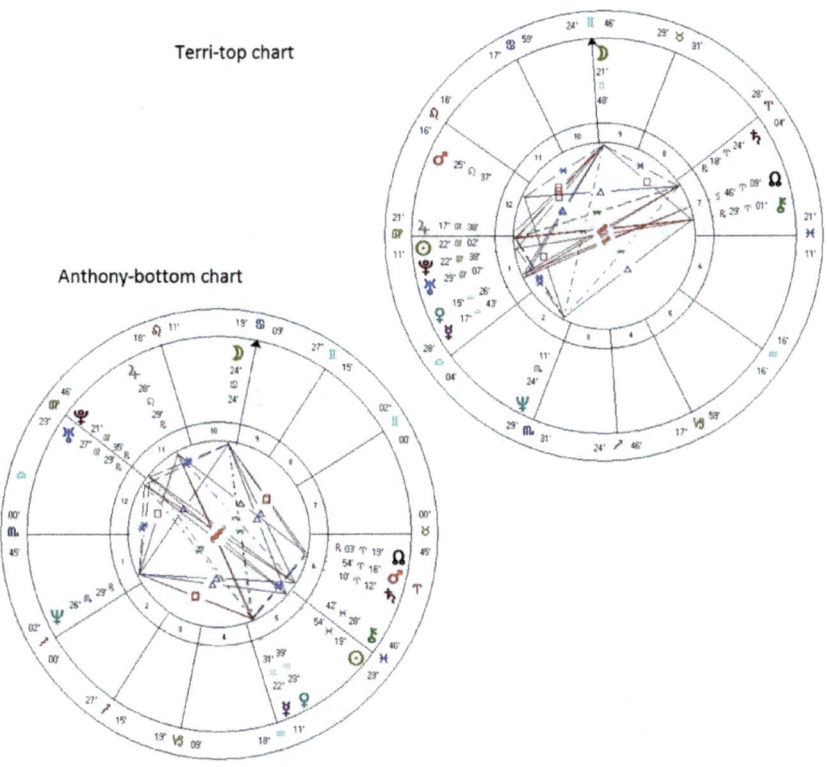

Chart: Marlin - *All his Elements are strong except Fire: Water (Moon conjunct Ascendant and Pluto in the 1st House) this is very strong; Air (Gemini Sun and Mercury); and Earth (Virgo Ascendant and three Planets in Virgo in the 1st House).*

Marlin

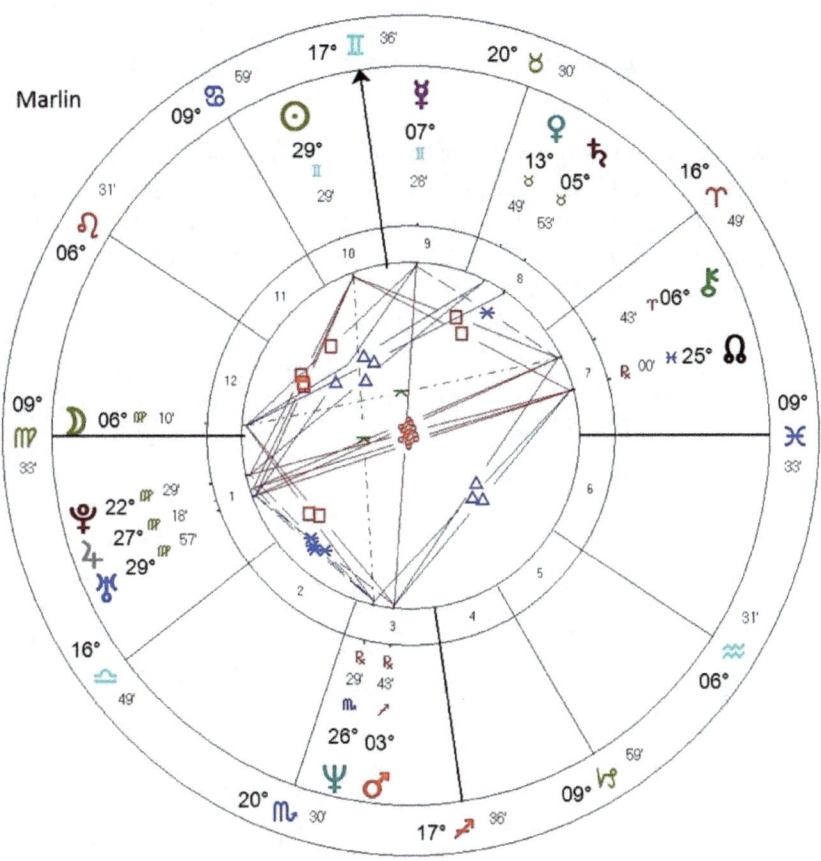

Chart: Katrina - *sexual abuse as a child, damage to sexual organs, problem with relationships. I included this chart because of its incredibly powerful Water 12th House and Air Libra Stellium. Five Planets, which is a large Stellium, Neptune is exalted in his own House, a Luminary, the Sun is involved and conjunct Mars and Mercury. She also has a watery Scorpio Ascendant.*

Her Moon is in Virgo in the 11th House: this suggests a need to serve and provide for others, which she did. The Mars-Sun Conjunction suggests physical abuse but there is no strong indicator of sexual abuse.

In all my years working with sexually abused individuals, I have yet to feel confident using astrology to predict sexual abuse. It is an issue that is far too important to play around with. I suggest you be careful too. Such psychological issues as sexual abuse will be covered in a future book.

Katrina

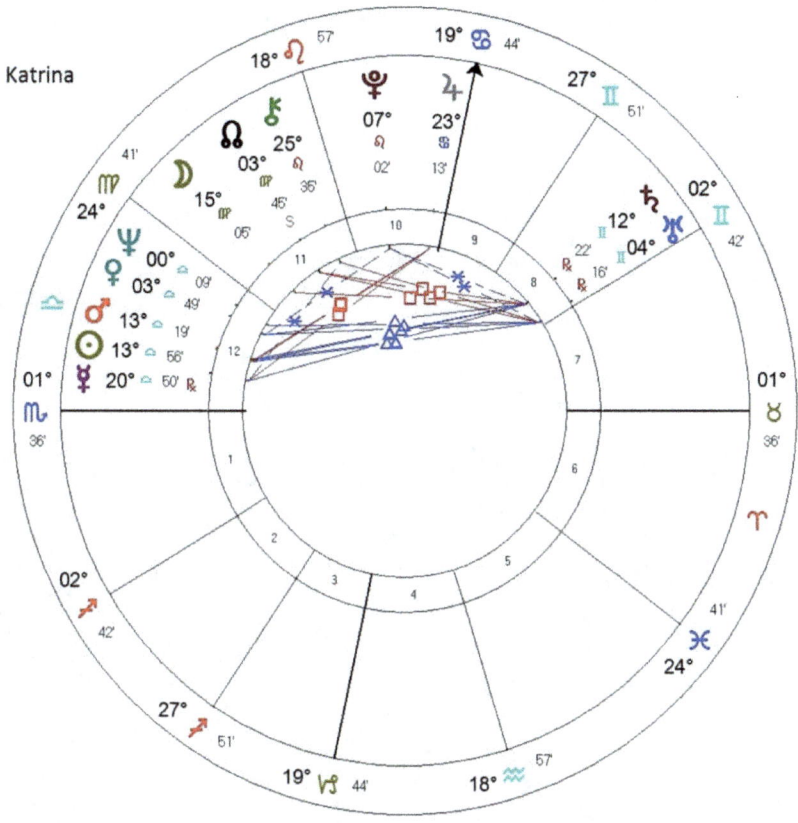

Chart: Berenice - *strong Water Element with Moon conjunct her Scorpio Ascendant, bladder cancer with Venus conjunct Neptune conjunct 12th House cusp in Libra.*

Berenice

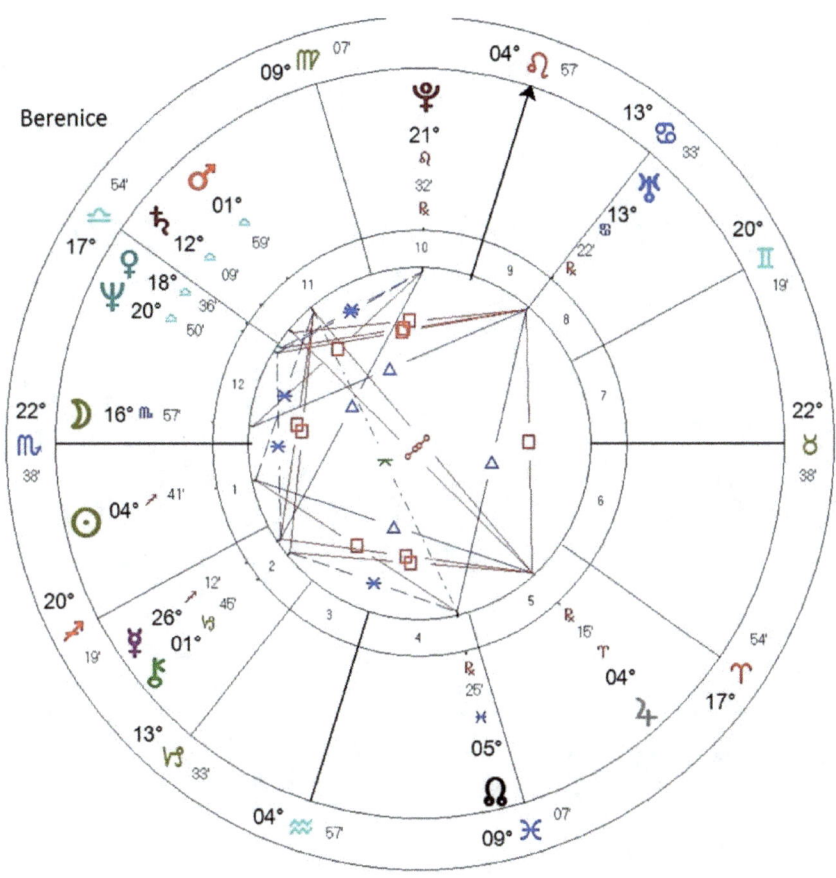

Chart: Jameson - *very watery, Pisces Ascendant with both Luminaries in the 12th House.*

Jameson

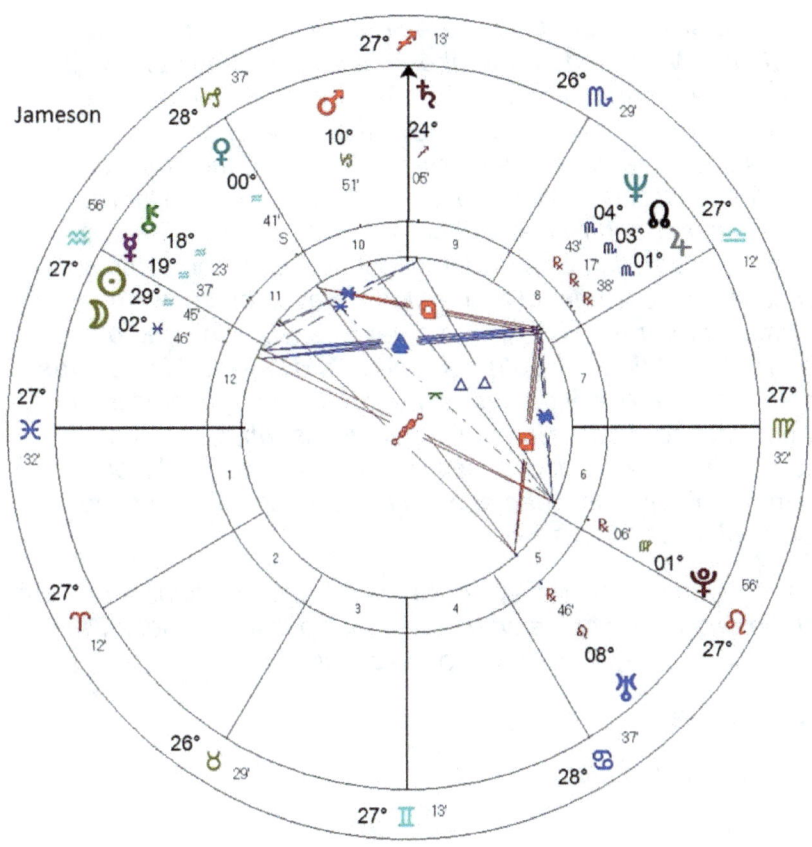

Lesson 4

Noel: *We are now at the final Element, Water, which is very emotional. We need to remember that emotions and physical symptoms go hand in hand, which is why astrology is so hard to use in diagnosis. If two people have the same chart they don't necessarily have the same illnesses. However, they may somatise (manifest physically) their stress into different but similar illnesses. For instance Moon issues can come out as asthma or colon issues (constipation or watery faeces) and a nervous stomach because both are related to the Moon. Have you known an asthma sufferer who doesn't also have constipation and other disturbed elimination? Both come from a distressed large intestine. The acupuncture meridian runs through both large intestine and lungs. Back to Water. Emotions, neediness, abandonment, passion, betrayal, jealousy, control, intensity, manipulation are all Water emotions and when expressed in a negative way, they can lead to physical illness.*

Even though we think of Water Signs as very emotional, they are not the ones to have the worst relationship issues, guess who do? Earth, Air or Fire? And only two guesses!

Student: *Fire.*

N - Close, next guess.

S - Damn. Air.

N - Yes correct. Air types are quite often out of touch with their feelings. So even though we say so much about the feelings of Water: jealousy and abandonment, for some reason they cope well enough. Air Signs, which of course means Ascendant, Sun, Moon or Stellium in Air or emphasis on the Air Houses or Air Signature have great difficulty coping with relationships. Of all my clients in counseling (and I can draw upon about 50 charts here), the Air ones have the worst track record.

Water: abandonment is a big time problem for Neptunians. For some reason, having a strong Neptune is not always about spirituality. It is about feeling disconnected and abandoned.

S - I can relate. People look at my chart and think I'm an addict. I'm not even an addictive personality. I have a Water heavy chart.

N - Where is your Neptune?

S - Sun Pisces, Moon Scorpio conjunct Neptune, Pluto Rising. They also tell me I'm psychic which I'm not. Intuitive, maybe. I'm also a very un-New-Agey astrologer.

N - *Hurrah for that, so am I. If you experience any Sign of dishonesty you turn away from that person. Is that correct?*

S - Exactly. So, yes, I don't talk all that spiritual mumbo-jumbo.

N - *Pluto rising is all about character. If people you meet are false you will smell it and move on.*

S - True. Are the Air dudes like that, too?

N - *Too much Air is more related to magical thinking, remember? And that is mumbo jumbo to us both. It is too easy to play esoteric astrology.*

S - That's a terrific insight about Air, the magical thinking.

N - *Yes. I am glad you can see it coming together.*

S - Tell me more about Water people.

N - *I like strong Pluto people. Like me, they don't muck about, they get straight to the point.*

S - Oh, wait, you spoke about Neptunians. Which do you consider the Water Planets? Moon, Neptune, Pluto?

N - *Yes.*

S - Ah ok.

N - *So back to umm, Water? Neptune.*

S - Yes.

N - *He is the God of emotions but not quite as deep as Pluto. Neptune is most closely related to abandonment and erosion. I use the word 'abandonment' a lot for him especially after he transited my Ascendant. Pluto is 'betrayal'. For instance if Pluto were square your Sun you would feel betrayed by your father. Not necessarily that you hate him but you will make sure that you avoid situations that lead to vulnerability and to possible betrayal. It could transfer to all authority or father figures which is the Sun in this instance. Does that make sense?*

S - Yes indeed.

N - Neptune, however, is abandonment, loneliness, loss, grief. Neptune square Sun could manifest as distrust and abandonment. One would feel that father is not there for you. He abandons you when you need him most. So there are subtle differences between the two and being Outer Planets and thus very powerful, they don't take prisoners.

S - So you feel you can't rely on your father. Gotcha.

N - So how would that equate with Neptune conjunct Moon?

S - A mother who can't be relied upon.

N - Does that sound true to you?

S - Yep.

N - OK, my thesis is sound. The two Outer Planets are very deep and painful when poorly aspected but even when they are not poorly aspected they are still painful. There is another side to Pluto.

S - Quite.

N - Fear. Not just ordinary fear but panic and fear of physical violence. If it is opposite Mars then you would say that the native fears being hurt or bashed and was often the victim of bullying at school. Pluto conjunct Sun could also be fear of father. Pluto / Moon fear of mother. Then there is the sexual side if it aspects Sun then father was sexually active in some way. If to the Moon, then it was mother who was sexually active. So Pluto is multi-dimensional. With all that activity, no wonder Pluto is also passion and intensity. In Pluto we also see health issues. Too much emphasis will seriously affect that area such as in a Conjunction with Mars. That could include sexual glands, organs, kidneys, blood, wounds, accidents.

Neptune is mysteries: mystery illness, flu symptoms, very much the flu and viruses. For some reason Neptune also weakens the native. They are too adaptive, too flexible, too considerate, too compliant, too forgiving, too nice. Eventually they pick up every known bug in the universe because they are not living their life but live for others.

S - Gosh yes, too compliant and forgiving. Cutting other people too much slack, definitely.

N - But Pluto wants to help you stop this slide into ill health. If he can't protect you he may internalise these intense, passionate feelings of outrage and you get sick. What House is your Moon?

S - 3rd

N - The conscious mind, excess thoughts and worry unless you can speak up for yourself. But perhaps that would be hard with Neptune trying to keep everyone happy. Pluto will be straining at his leash because he just wants to bite those rude people. If you let him off his leash you could become fearful that he will harm someone. So here we have the Plutonic fear of your own power to hurt, maim, damage or destroy verbally. So what do you do? You keep Pluto in a cage. He is too dangerous to let out because it's just not sociable to say nasty things. However there are safe ways to let off Pluto's steam. Can you give me a hint?

S - Pound rocks? Competitive sport where you can kill your opponent. Martial arts (I just started tai chi again).

N - Hey, just like me! Do you want a hint?

S - Yes.

N - Just think why many people marry and not for the money either.

S - Oh that.

N - Yes it's 'that' sex thing and sex is kundalini. Kundalini is touching the spirit and the spirit is Neptune. Plutonic energy is necessary for spiritual union. His tension is then translated through tai chi and kundalini meditations into becoming one with the great mother's womb, the universe and eventually Neptune. Ta da!

We could say that people with strong Pluto have strong sexual urges which enables them to reach their goal which is re-union with the universe. Neptune is the vision and dream of the womb, the universe and Pluto gets you there. I started to astral travel six months after beginning tai chi. I have Pluto conjunct Sun, Venus, and Mars in the 8th House. I had no choice in the matter. I also have Neptune conjunct MC and that contributed to my journey to the universe. This search for spirit is certainly part of Water's domain.

S - So you're a Neptune-Pluto like me.

N - Neptune is sextile Pluto, Sun, Venus, Mars all in Leo and Neptune is in Libra.

S - Leo gives Pluto some "lift".

N - Yes he sure does. Now let's look at the first two charts, **Terri and Anthony.** They were once married to each other

S - Ah!

N - Even though Terri has little Water, I wanted to show you the Pluto 1st House and I didn't know that this is where your Pluto was, too...

S - It's actually in the 12th but closely conjunct the Ascendant.

N - Ah even more powerful. With Terri we have Fire, Earth, Air and Water all in the 1st House. Your Pluto is made more powerful because it is applying to the cusp of the 1st. applying Planets are always more powerful than separating.

S - It's retrograde.

N - Hmm, Terri may be a bit easier to read than you. The influence of Pluto on Terri is quite powerful, exact conjunct Sun. Oh and 1 degree separating from the Ascendant. So he is tough and hard on her. In fact Terri has too much in that 1st House to adequately delineate. It's all mixed up and she has no idea where she is going. Her ex-husband Anthony, has interesting things too. Look at his cusps: 12th 6th and 10th. Tell me what you see?

S - He has Scorpio Rising, Mars the ruler conjunct Saturn.

N - I use Pluto as ruler of Scorpio.

S - Cancer Moon conjunct MC, quincunx Mercury and Venus, co-rulers of the 12th House, Mercury-Venus opposite Jupiter, Pisces Sun conjunct Chiron, opposing Pluto-Uranus on cusp of 12th, yeesh.

N - Yeesh indeedy. We could say that he is way too watery with that Sun in Pisces conjunct Chiron. The wound is by his father with Scorpio Ascendant and Pluto its ruler on the 12th cusp, conjunct Uranus. This is very hard on him. In fact any Planets conjunct the 12th cusp opens up the 12th House of fear of abandonment. Opposite Sun and Chiron shows more abandonment issues.

S - Also Neptune in Scorpio focal in Fixed T-Square with the Mercury/Venus-Jupiter Opposition.

N - *Sure is, good work. I missed that. We add Saturn singleton conjunct Mars and we have anger / frustration with nowhere to go. Actually it goes out through the Square to Moon.*

Here we have the picture. Very emotional, wounded, fearful of abandonment and he gets angry when his wife frustrates him. His anger sits on a mountain of abandonment.

We worked on his Moon, Mars and Saturn in trance. The Moon was a Goddess, she was untouchable. Saturn had Mars imprisoned in a cage. Mars was so angry and Saturn was given the job of cage keeper. He is still in need of help but he does martial arts which helps. With a wife that has so many personal issues herself their relationship was doomed to fail.

S - There's a grand Water Trine, Moon-Neptune-Sun/Chiron.

N - *The Trine is nice, yes, but this only means that he can have fun. Drink a lot, party but get to the deep personal intimacy and you unleash fear and impotence (loss of power).*

S - It must make it hard for him to introspect on his pain.

N - *Exactly. Remember, the key to a person is their conflicts. Find their conflicts and you find how they spend all their energy: trying to resolve it, successfully or not so successfully.*

S - Makes sense.

N - *They tend not to even notice their strengths like the grand Trine. It is just a talent that they have but never notice it.*

S - I could have probably predicted the separation emotional problems. Their Saturns aspect each other terribly.

N - *Ready for the next chart?*

S - Yep!

N - **Marlin:** *Pluto in the 1st, Moon applying to the Ascendant, Jupiter, our old friend, in the first too with Uranus. I know this guy's health problems so it is a little easier for us today. What would you say his conflicts are? Just give me two or three.*

S - Doesn't feel safe being himself? (The 1st House group square the Sun).

N - *Wow, great, and his sexual orientation is gay. This may help our understanding, let's see.*

S - Ascendant ruler Mercury opposite Mars: fear of violence to his person?

N - *Yes, correct and his mother actively brainwashed him against his father.*

S - Right. The Moon makes a T-Square to Mars-Mercury.

N - *They were separated for many years and so he grew up to dislike his father. Thus the T-Square. He hated his mother too. She was always in his pocket. Wouldn't let him grow up. Too much Moon, applying to Ascendant, the focal point of T-Square. But he was passionate and driven, 1st House stuff. When he became emotional, he became confused - 3rd House issues and Moon / Pluto 1st.*

S - Question: you've mentioned control issues in connection with both Earth and Water, is there a different slant with Earth vs. Water?

N - *Yes, Earth is about power battles, to be in charge of possessions and the physical self; with Water it is Pluto and control over life. Everything is a life or death struggle for that control with Water especially Pluto. Pluto will go down fighting. Everything is a battle to the death for Pluto; while with Earth it is: 'if I don't win I will give up and try again later'. To understand Earth, imagine someone is trying to take your train set or Barbie doll. With Water, it's losing the oral 'love object', your partner.*

S - Mmm, can you give me an example?

N - *Earth is potty training: the control of physical objects involving the traits of meanness, ungenerous, collects things but doesn't display them, hoarding, selfish. They can be quite unpleasant.*

S - So it's control of things rather than people?

N - *Yes. With Pluto it is passion, they are not mean at all. Pluto says, "If I believe in a cause I will die for that cause." Earth would never do that. Pluto is not mean just passionate to the extreme.*

Add the word 'death' and there is a whole heap of difference between the two.

S - Isn't dependence the dark side of Water?

N - Yes, there is a lot going on in Water. There can be life and death struggles below the surface, no one sees it. It is also about connecting with the unconscious: Neptune is spirit and Pluto is death (and life after death); Moon is being a baby again. Does that help?

S - Mmm, still wondering.

N - They do intermix their definitions: all will be revealed in time through this course. Let's look at your Pluto: you are passionate about the things you love?

S - Yes.

N - You might not die for it but you certainly feel very passionate about it especially if someone criticises your passion. You may even get very deeply hurt too.

S - Yes.

N - If you were a soldier all that your general would have to do is make you believe passionately in something, then you would fight like the devil.

S - Probably.

N - Next chart: **Marlin** - Chronic Fatigue Syndrome from very low tone in his large intestines. This comes from his Virgo Stellium and his 1st House.

S - Right.

N - He worries too much. Neptune and Mars in the 3rd House opposite Mercury, and the Sun in Gemini. This focuses on Neptune in the thinking 3rd House and Air. He has a partying lifestyle, Jupiter first with Uranus and Sun in Gemini, that leads to a poor diet, lack of sleep and susceptible to illness. Participating in anal intercourse means he needs to watch for his colon health and STD's. We look at Marlin later in our lessons too.

Now we look at **Katrina:** terribly abused by father, relatives, visitors, brothers, sexual and physical, very nasty stuff here. Look at the 12th House. It is loaded and Jupiter on his MC. Pluto is there, too. All that Water and Fire: alcohol and bad relationships. She spent time in a mental institution and had a lesbian relationship there. No doubt that helped her with her 12th House abandonment issues. She is now married to an alcoholic. Her mother forced her to have an abortion as a teenager when she was pregnant with her father's baby. She was sent to a Catholic Convent to have it aborted. She said that it was the worst experience of loss in her life. Abandonment, abuse and psychological illness and then suicidal. That 12th House dominance can be very nasty: falling apart from the inside.

Next chart, sorry to rush, but time is running out. **Jameson:** loaded 12th again and the 8th. Saturn on his MC a difficult mix of Pisces and Aquarius in the 12th, mixed up thoughts, suicidal over relationships. Pluto is also opposite Sun and Moon so cancer may be his major problem in later years. Not because Pluto is in the 6th not at all, but because of the loaded 12th House opposite Pluto.

Berenice, her bladder almost died from too much coffee and wine. She had an operation for bladder and womb recently. I can't remember why I put her in? I better pass the ball to you now. Any questions or comments?

S - Scorpio Rising?

N - Yes! Of course!

S - Moon conjunct Scorpio Ascendant from 12th, square Pluto.

N - Yes. Moon rules the female organs.

S - Venus (sole dispositor) ruling the 12th and in the 12th. Saturn-Venus-Neptune in the 12th House conjunct the 12th cusp and square Uranus in Cancer in the 8th.

N - Yep, you're doing better than me.

S - That's about it for Water.

N - We'll look at Berenice and the others in more detail in later lessons, too.

S - Will we talk about specific disease Signatures when we get to the end of the course? Will I be able to look at a chart and come up with possible illnesses the person might have?

N - Yes, because you are already an accomplished astrologer, you will - but it ain't easy. That skill takes a lot of practice. The *material in this course will give you the necessary foundations you will need to develop further and become an expert in health astrology. You can also take my AstroPsychology course.*

S - Someone asked me a question about the daughter of a friend. She's sick and the doctors can't figure out what's wrong with her.

N - We should look at her chart for the next lesson, please send me the details by email.

S - Okay.

N - I shall await your email and we can look at it using the Elements and Inner Planets and more if we have time.

Chapter 5

Constitutional health - Part 1 - Planets

The natal chart holds the keys we need to understand our constitutional health, the strengths and weaknesses we were born with. In later lessons we will look at how, through Transit and Progression, we can expect a weakening or a challenge to certain aspects of our health and how it may manifest. Traditionally, each Planet, Sign and House is assigned body parts, herbs and fluids. Let us first look at the traditional approach of constitutional health.

The Planets - Health Keywords and Rulerships

The Planets are, of course, similar to the Signs that they rule. There is also a crossing over of their traditional organs and body systems. With practice, you will find it easier to delineate them. Included are the traditional medicinal herbs for the 7 visible Planets.

Sun - Heart, back, spinal column, general immunity and vitality.

Chamomile, Rosemary, Eyebright

Moon - Body fluids, oedema, lymph, female organs, breasts, digestive system, lymphatic system, stomach, oesophagus, liver, pancreas, small intestines, gall bladder.

Willow, Watercress, Poppy, Cucumber, White Roses

Mercury - Respiration, lungs, brain, sensory nervous system, thyroid gland, mental processes, fingers, hands, five senses.

Caraway, Lavender

Venus - Throat, viral infections, thymus gland, throat infections, kidneys, lumbar region, ovaries, sense of touch.

Coltsfoot, Woodsage, Alder, Elder, Wild Thyme

Mars - Muscles, head, adrenal glands, smell and taste, urogenital region, blood, encephalitis, fevers, bleeding, accidents. Mars natally shows where the native burns up the most energy. It is limited by the Sign it is in however.. For example Mars in a Water Sign is not as energetic as when in the other three Elements.

Bryonia, Hops

Jupiter - Addictions, liver, pituitary gland, blood disorders, obesity, thighs, feet, growth.

Cinquefoil, Hyssop, Red Roses, Henbane

Saturn - Gall bladder, spleen, skin rashes, hair, teeth and bones, joints, muscle tone, asthma, body's defense systems. Saturn shows us reality, we can't escape Saturn. I think that because he is the only Planet that is totally Earth, he needs to be three times as strong, which is why he acts so powerfully in our charts. Saturn shows limits, physical as well as metaphysical. When we reach the threshold of these limits he can manifest as depression, sometimes a physical illness. You can bet that it is a long illness requiring a long convalescence.

Comfrey, Ivy, Hemlock, Belladonna

Chiron - Not enough research has been done on this asteroid belt Dwarf Planet. Perhaps it is the immune system, psychological health and overall healing potential. Chiron natally shows where the fundamental psychological wound comes from, what it is associated with and how it can be healed—in association with other points of the chart. It points to psychological as well as physical wounds. For instance, if in the 1st House, it is more often the sense organs, eyes, ears, sensory nerves, etc. and shows that the native may be emotionally scarred by their wound. Similar to Pluto in action. Please note that transiting Chiron can trigger, or contribute to, physical and psychological health problems. No traditional herbs.

Uranus - Circulatory system, nerves, nervous system, epilepsy, parathyroid. Uranus shows us where tension resides, as well as, the need for freedom. It may manifest as anxiety which can also present as hyperactivity. Aquarius or Uranus can sometimes be seen highlighted in the charts of alcoholics or drug addicts. For instance, a Uranus - Moon Conjunction can indicate irritability with older women and the native's mother. It can also manifest as irritable stomach or bowel, digestive problems, etc. particularly when their mother is around. It can also contribute to excessive drinking so that the native can calm their racing thoughts and their excessive worry. As an Air Planet, Uranus can contribute to problems related to stress and worry. It is also the Planet of the genius mind and non-linear thinking. No traditional herbs.

Neptune - General health, thalamus, pineal gland, fluids, glandular imbalance, infections. Neptune often manifests as colds, influenza and fluid retention. I don't find that he is singularly associated with alcohol and drugs as is stated in most mass produced astrology books. A strong Neptune or Pisces can indicate depression when the native has strong feelings of abandonment. This abandonment and the ensuing depression can be the force that drives them to drink. As opposed to Uranus or other Air types who drink to quiet and slow their mind to relax and sleep, the Water types drink because they are sad, lost, grieving and depressed. Neptune health issues are related to fluids, influenza type illnesses, mysterious illnesses, psychological illness particularly described above, sadness and abandonment, rather than any true psychosis. When in Progression it can trigger such things as confused thoughts and inattention, inability to focus, particularly on the Ascendant and in aspect to Mercury. No traditional herbs.

Pluto - Testes, ovaries, sex organs, prostrate, pancreas, metabolism, elimination, kundalini, libido and sex drive, energy healing, astral travel, overall healing potential. Pluto is a very psychologically driven Planet. When found on the Angles or conjunct the Luminaries and Inner Planets, he may manifest physically as well. Anything in the 6th House can manifest physically, but don't think that Pluto in the 6th is always cancer as many do, he may indicate a low functioning immune system or fear of illness. The fear he generates can reduce resilience, which may contribute to illness. Pluto in Transit can be very damaging, this is often when someone goes to a psychologist for counseling. If you know someone in crisis and they have a Pluto transiting a Luminary, Inner Planet or an Angle, then suggest they go and talk to someone. Pluto seeks to destroy what is unhealthy in their life, particularly old negative programs and belief systems. Unfortunately, his method is extremely heavy handed and can cause severe long lasting health problems. No traditional herbs.

Natal Planets in Health - Summary and Discussion

Sun and Moon, the Luminaries are both quite happy to be anywhere in our psyche. When poorly aspected, we try to understand the combinations of their planetary networks, their aspects, to decide just how this impacts the native's health. Sun or Moon by themselves are not a health problem, we can't get too much Sun or too much Moon in our charts. The problem is what they touch by Conjunction and Opposition, with the Angles and any of the Planets. When conjunct or opposed by an Outer Planet in particular, they will take on the health issues of that Planet. In some ways we could say they amplify those health issues, for both good and bad. For instance, Moon conjunct Saturn, can lead to depression, sadness, osteoporosis, weak stomach and irritable digestive system. It can also strengthen, providing a protective factor for the native by improving their resilience. Mostly, I look for more than one single factor. Just Moon conjunct Saturn is not enough for me to say that there will be health issues, I would look for Capricorn factors and Cancer factors to back this up. If no other factors can be found, I would probably consider that the Moon-Saturn Conjunction is a positive aspect of the chart and one that enhances their health and resilience.

Mercury is the Planet of the mind, the conscious mind, thoughts, ideas and plans. Neptune leans towards the unconscious and dreams. When Mercury is over-emphasised in a chart, we would notice racing thoughts, confused mental processes and difficulty forming words and sentences, adding numbers, etc. We sometimes notice this when Mercury goes retrograde every few months, when people's well-laid plans fall apart, communications fail and electrical appliances break. Mercury can also be seen in health in connection with sensory failures, hearing and seeing. However, I am more inclined to look at his mental health implications, though minor, they are there. Mercury mental health issues are nowhere near as problematic as the Outer Planet issues, so please don't be too worried if you have Mercury powerfully placed in your chart. I have Mercury conjunct Moon in Virgo in my 8th House and his activity allows me to engage people, to chit chat and talk, ask questions, listen attentively, etc. If anything, he enhances my other qualities rather than weakens them. If, however, he were conjunct say Uranus, then it could indicate excess mental stress, worry and disturbed sleep that would be a problem. So watch out for Outer Planet Conjunctions and Oppositions to natal Mercury.

Venus is the Planet of relationships, wealth and cash flow. If we wish to just stick to health, we would consider its House placement and any aspects it forms with the Luminaries and Outer Planets. Its Sign placement indicates its tone of action particularly as it rules both an Air Sign (Libra) and an Earth Sign (Taurus). Her versatility is enormous, which may be why she contributes so many positive qualities and traits to our lives. Her main contribution in health analysis is kidneys and throat, throat infections and voice box, speaking. Although Mercury is the Planet of communication, it is Venus who draws people towards us and engages them with her voice and her charms. I think I would also give her rulership over the thyroid because she rules the throat and overall harmony, thyroid rules cellular harmony. Venus is like an orchestra, so too is the thyroid.

Mars shows where the native burns up their energy, he is impacted by the Sign and House he resides in. For instance, Mars in a Water House is less physical, it slows his activity, energy and drive. He manifests more in line with the Element of that House or Sign. I consider Mars quite limited in his expression of his energy force, he is more a line of energy, directed like a laser beam, he doesn't have the finesse and versatility of Venus. His energy has a single purpose and too much can be detrimental to health, not enough has a similar effect. If you see a strong Mars in a chart, first consider his Sign and House placement before you look at his aspects to other Planets. He adds energy or he can be confused and directionless, similar to a confused Neptune. Mars needs direction, if he doesn't have it in the natal chart then it needs to be given to him. This can be done in meditation, through working with the other archetypes who will be able to guide his extremely powerful form of energy. You can download my free ebook on working in trance with your archetypes from my web site:- www.plutoscave.com

Jupiter wants to be happy all the time. He will join organisations just to be able to help out and make someone else happy. Jupiterians gain great satisfaction when they can express their knowledge and generosity of spirit. Sometimes they will drink too much or take drugs to get this same satisfaction, or maybe they will just overindulge in everything like food and sex. Jupiter tends to bring on their own health problems through poor lifestyle choices and as such watch the liver, it's his main organ, next is the gall bladder. Many health problems arising from over-indulgence can be laid at the feet of Jupiter.

Saturn is an amazing Planet, it triggers events every seven or so years as it Transits through the zodiac and around your chart. Its most pressing health needs, however, are shown in its natal placement. The House Saturn resides in indicates exactly where you need to tidy and clean up your life. Saturn brings order and structure, if the House is Water then you need to focus and structure your emotional health; Earth is physical health; for Fire it is spiritual and if in an Air Sign, it is intellectual and mental health. Saturn is structure, so look for physical body structure, bones, teeth, joints and posture. As it has a tendency to weaken other Planets, we would look at its Conjunctions and Oppositions to Luminaries and Personal Planets.

Chiron shows the native's fundamental wound, its aspects and House placement shows what this fundamental wound may be associated with. Chiron is most powerful when conjunct a Luminary or Personal Planet, Sun, Moon, Mercury, Venus, Mars or Jupiter or conjunct the Ascendant or Midheaven. Little is known about Chiron yet, but what we do know is that he is powerfully related to health and healing. Natives with Chiron strongly placed are often wounded healers themselves and have an innate ability to tap into the source of this power. They also understand, from first-hand experience, how to heal others.

Uranus indicates tension and a drive for freedom; if it is in an Air House or conjunct Mercury, it will indicate a drive for freedom of speech; if in Fire it will be freedom of space; in Water, freedom to feel and express their feelings; and if in an Earth House, it indicates where the native seeks to experience freedom to use their physical belongings. In health astrology, it often indicates mental irritability, particularly by Conjunction and Opposition to a Luminary, Inner Planet or conjunct an Angle. Watch for mental stress and excess worrying when in powerful Conjunction natally and in Transit.

Neptune in the natal chart shows by its House placement where the native experiences mysterious illnesses, where they feel most abandoned or depressed; and by Conjunction and Opposition with Luminaries, Inner Planets or conjunct the Angles, how this will manifest in their lives. Neptune's action is so subtle that most natives never know it is happening. As the ruler of Pisces and the most watery of all the Planets, Neptune's action is just like water, he dissolves and erodes our stuck habits. He washes slowly and inexorably until we give in and let go of our pride, our negative habits and our prejudices. His are often the worst of Transits, as he sneaks up and washes the ground from beneath you. Of all the Planets, meditation and dream work are critical to understand and manage his energy.

Pluto is perhaps the most psychological of all the Planets, natally he shows psychological stress or limitations. By House placement and Conjunction or Opposition with Luminaries, Inner Planets and Conjunctions to the Angles, he can indicate where his controlling and domineering behaviour and fearfulness resides. When working with Pluto, one must realise that he rules kundalini and all life forces. By learning to tap into your own life force through tai chi, chi kung, yoga and tantra, you will begin to understand his role in your life. I astral traveled once I began learning tai chi and doing specific chi / life-force enhancing meditations. On one occasion, I met the archetype, Kundalini, and he told me to use it more. I had no trouble flowing his life-force through my body. But be careful, he will burn you if you don't respect and honour his power.

Gale

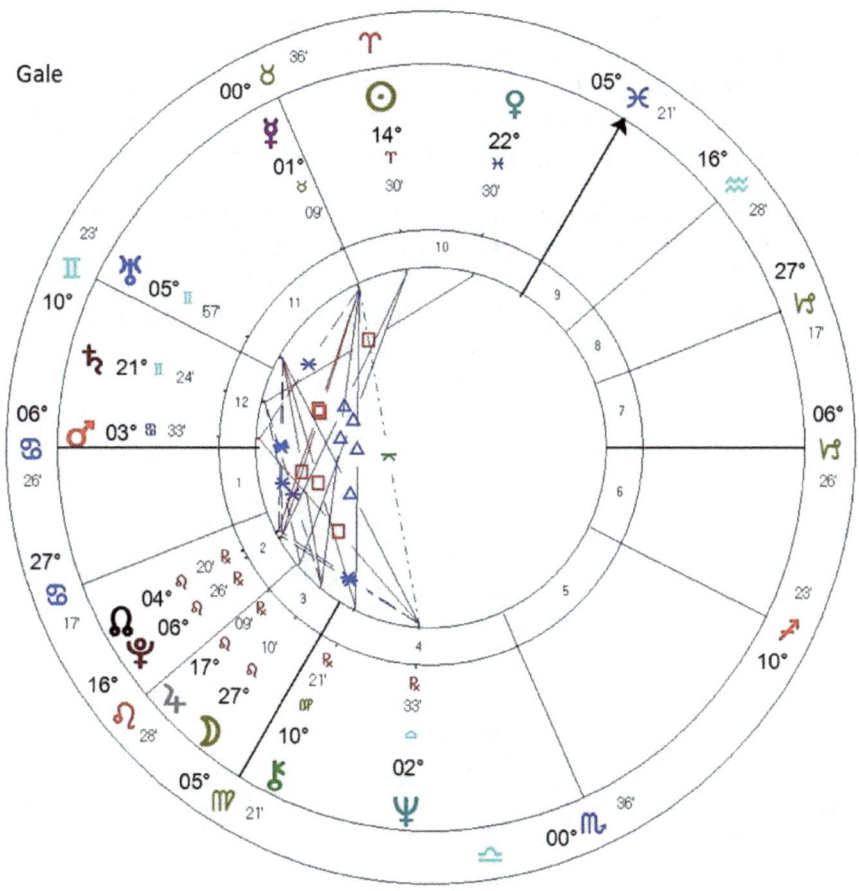

Chart: Gale - *she was an astrologer, a driven lady who loved her family. She had a lot of Fire in her chart, Leo Stellium, Aries Sun and Moon in Leo. Notice that both Luminaries were in Fire. That is important.*

Mars was the trigger Planet, sitting within Michel Gauquelin's sector, within a 3° orb applying to her watery Cancer Ascendant. This placement made it the most powerful Planet in her chart, and it too is a Fire Planet (Mars also rules Aries). Moon in Leo conjunct another Fire Planet, Jupiter, overly emphasises Fire once again.

The two Luminaries, Sun and Moon, are always very important indicators of what the native spends most of their time resolving and doing. Their House placement indicates WHERE this occurs, in Gale's case her career and her communication. As she was an astrologer, her Luminaries were perfectly placed.

Chart: Amanda - *Pisces Moon and a mini Pisces Stellium in the 9th House; Sun in Gemini in the 12th House with Air Gemini on the Ascendant; Venus in the 1st House. Abandonment and betrayal by mother and sexual abuse by father. Sexual health issues.*

Amanda

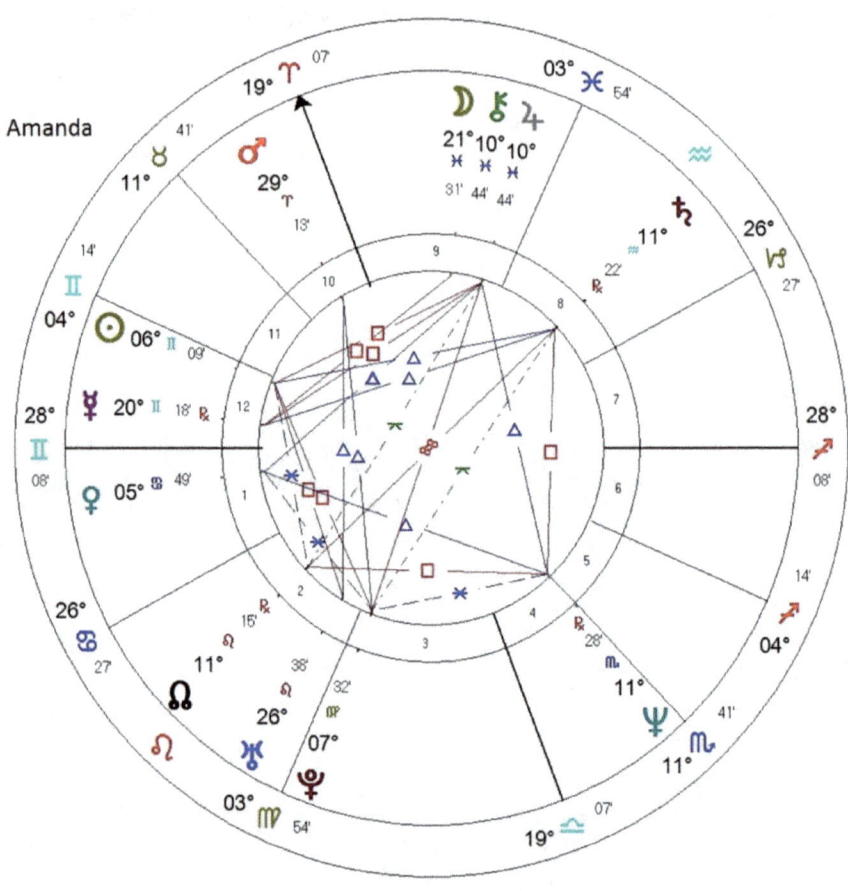

Chart: Leah - *deaf, abusive father, vertigo and a fantastically free lady. Conflicted Moon opposite Chiron, Sun in Libra opposite Saturn, 4th House Stellium and Gemini Ascendant. More information in our transcripts.*

Leah

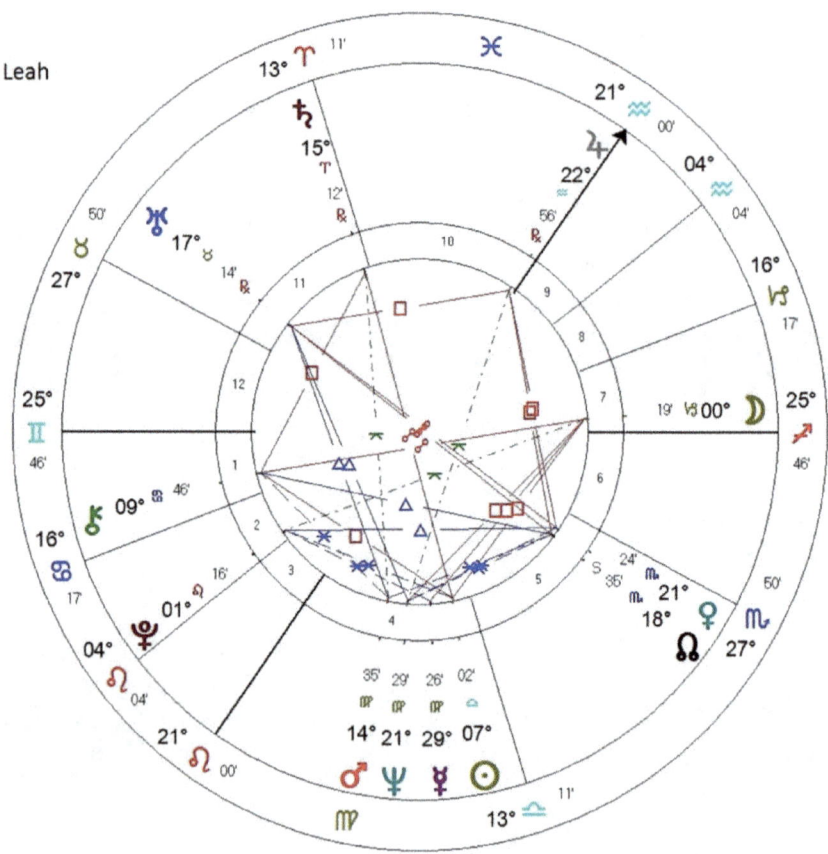

Chart: Laura - *Saturn conjunct her Virgo Ascendant, Moon in Gemini and Venus MC in Gemini, strong Air, Sun conjunct Mars in Taurus in the 8th House shows impatience and interest in the occult. Neptune in the 1st House suggests this as well as influencing her decisions about relationships with that strong Venus and Moon in Gemini (denial). A combination of strong Elements Air, Earth and Fire with some Water, makes it difficult to delineate sometimes.*

Laura

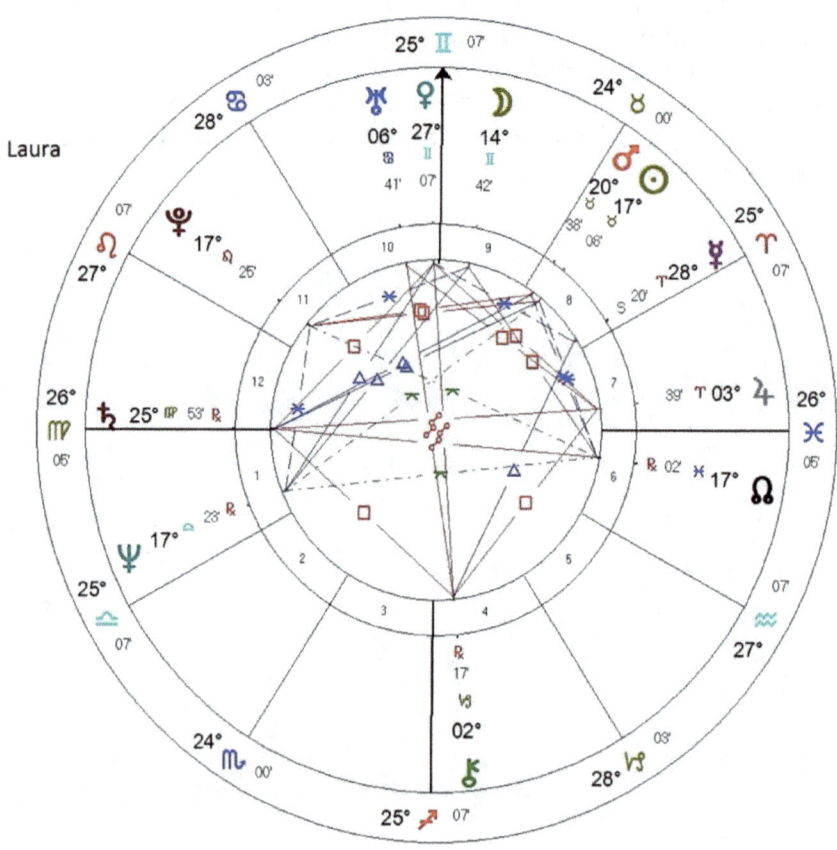

Chart: JR - *young dancer with health issues and what may be an autoimmune disease, anxiety or just super sensitive. More in our lesson transcripts.*

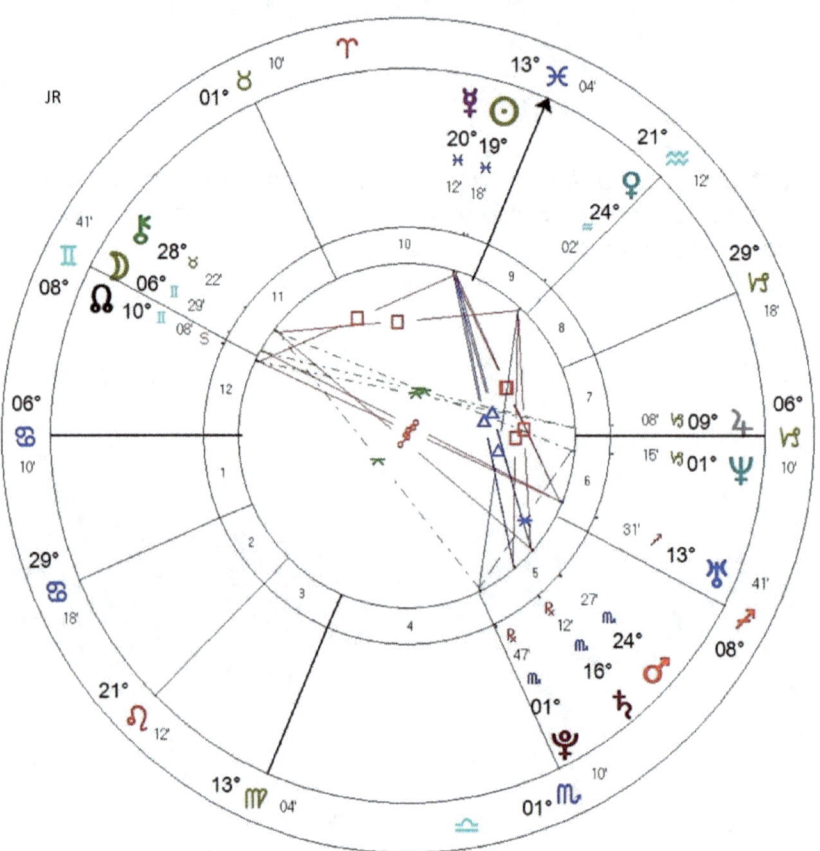

Lesson 5

Noel: *Back to the Planets*

Student: Yes!

N - First thing to remember when practicing health astrology is that sometimes people do things that defy astrology: like smoking, drinking, exposure to electrical fields and radiation, toxic medications. These are things we have no control over. Can you think of any others?

S - Recreational drugs, hit by a car, petrochemical toxins, cosmic rays while flying in airplanes, etc.

N - Yes. These are things that we can't account for and which do not show up in the native's birth chart and often not even in their progressed charts. The natal chart shows constitutional strengths and weaknesses. A good astrologer should see their weaknesses, not necessarily their accidents, murders, injuries, exposures, etc. that will occur in modern daily life. Having said that, let's look at what we do have. The Planets natally: Sun is the heart, solar energy and solar plexus, strength, but I am not sure the medical astrology rulerships necessarily fit today. I struggle to connect with the Sun ruling the back but that's what the books on traditional medical astrology always say. Back would also be Saturn I would think, as it is the centre of the skeleton. The Sun as a symbol of universal strength shows immunity and vitality but so does Pluto. So as you can see we have blends of qualities much like how the Elements blend and blur their traits and qualities.

Moon: I always see the qualities of the Moon much clearer than that of the Sun. It is so clearly feminine, more so than Venus. Moon rules the female monthly cycle, ovaries, womb, female organs, though they say that Pluto also rules sexual organs. So they might just have to share this organ. Breasts are an easy one and we can see in Transits to natal Moon when the breasts are extra sensitive. Often fluid lumps occur during Transits and Lunations. It also rules the stomach, the digestive system and fluids like the lymph system.

Mercury should be most focused on the nerves, mental processes and what else? Respiration? Why respiration and lungs? I must research this one day. As you can see, there is so much to learn about the correspondences, what rules what can be very confusing.

Venus: throat and kidneys. I would also suggest Venus and Jupiter rule thyroid but traditionally it's Mercury. Mars is simple: blood and guts, knives and surgery, fevers, heat and temperatures.

S - Muscles, adrenaline.

N - Yes and sitting on the kidneys is the adrenal gland. So Mars is also involved with kidneys but so too is Venus.

S - Yes, as in Chinese medicine

N - Hey, that is absolutely right. Good one. We know that heat needs Water to cool it thus temperature and fevers rely on Mars. I use the philosophy of traditional Chinese medicine, too. It's a good mix and you know some Chinese healing, too. If urine is too strong, it suggests not enough water and the kidneys become irritated. Thus water, kidneys and Mars come together. Jupiter: lord of addictions, alcohol, work, sex, gambling, dope and escapism, much reflects on the liver to detoxify these toxins, pituitary gland, now why him? Guess...

S - Master gland, regulates everything.

N - Exactly! He is such a big Planet that he must be involved with something big and not just obesity. Saturn: funny how he regulates muscle tone too, this is spleen and pancreas, which in Chinese medicine also rules muscle tone. Saturn regulates many things just like the public service. I like Saturn. He reminds me of standing in line or waiting for a phone connection for hours.

S - I detest Saturn but then again I'm a Jovian. Truth is just truth. You can't have opinions about truth.

N - I am Saturn ruled. He is the Lord of my chart so I have no choice but to bow to him.

S - Life must be a lot easier for you then.

N - I have trouble with Jupiter because he squares Saturn and they don't get along. This means Saturn puts Jupiter in the deep freeze when I have work to do. All work and no play. Asthma, did you see that one?

S - Yeah, constriction of bronchial tubes.

N - In Chinese medicine, the lung meridian runs through the large intestines and many people who have asthma also have skin problems. This appears to be low energy in bowels: wastes stay way too long and ferments. They turn toxic and enter the lymph system. The body wisdom pushes the waste out through the skin. The parallels go on and on. Maybe Saturn as the Earthiest Planet is involved with large intestines and lungs, too.

Chiron: psychological wound, immune system perhaps? Maybe, we do get some clues when he is placed in the 1st House where he sometimes manifests physically by affecting the sense organs, eyes, ears, etc. These are also 'fundamental' wounds, ones we carry throughout our lifetime. A fundamental wound might be hearing loss. It is not just physical but it is also emotional. Or some disease that cripples and we have to deal with the laughter, jokes, put downs, humiliation, etc.

So Chiron is very important. Without coming to terms with our illness or with Chiron, we might never heal. It could be just the straw that breaks our back.

Uranus is circulation and brain chemistry. Too much of this can lead to a mental breakdown. So mental health plus nervous disorders come into his realm. Miscarriages may also involve Uranus (he is speed, electric, lightning fast).

Neptune: water, fluids and the flu. Neptune rules mysterious illnesses. Thus viruses and bacteria and sometimes alcohol but that is only if there are other triggers. We go to his keyword 'abandonment' to discover if the native feels abandoned and sad, to see if they turn to alcohol. With Jupiter, it is just an addiction and he wants to get high.

Pluto: my favourite and yours. I always think of the sex bits, sex organs, for Pluto. He includes regeneration, overheating due to over-excitement, chi and kundalini, astral travel, chi healing, Out Of Body, tantra, sex organs. Too much Pluto may lead to ovarian, cervix, prostate and testical problems, especially when triggered by Transit. We chatted a bit last time on him. And so we have the Planets.

OK, my student of astrological healing, what issues could come up with that list?

S - Which list? Pluto's list? Philosophical issues? Oh, just what you said before about the uncertainty of rulerships.

N - Darn right! Not enough research and too many overlaps.

S - I did some research on colour preferences and I found it all had to do with focal Planets in the chart rather than the Signs or Elements.

N - *That's an interesting find. I want to hear this.*

S - I'm wondering: if we get into a mess in medical astrology with rulerships for both the Signs and the Planets, maybe it's really one or the other.

N - *I agree. There is a distinction between Signs, Planets and Houses but should they be distinct or should they be overlapping. Is it OK to overlap? That is a topic to be researched and you have already started that research. Focal Planets are important anyway. No focus, no conflict and so no interest to resolve anything. We need to find the conflict / focal Planets and then we know what the native is thinking about. Once we know their thoughts, we know what they worry about and if we know their worries we know their weaknesses and that can be translated into physical health and personality issues, mental health. Thus your research is vital to all astrologers so keep doing it.*

S - Richard Idemon took an approach to chart analysis that began with focal Planets. He focused on singletons and missing Elements / qualities and determined that that's where the energy would be drawn. He could do quite an analysis before he'd even looked at a single aspect.

N - *I like that approach. In fact that is what we are doing or will be doing: find the conflict then you have the person. A singleton and particularly an 'unaspected' Planet is an incredibly 'wild card' or psychological factor in a chart. Please where did you find this?*

S - His books. Especially 'The Magic Thread'. The other is 'Through the Looking Glass.' They're both transcripts of seminars. Idemon didn't write any books.

N - *That's right. I read that in the introduction of 'Through The Looking Glass'. He sounds like my sort of astrologer.*

S - Thought so.

N - *We need to look at some charts now.* **Gale:** *we see Water and Fire; Cancer Ascendant and Mars conjunct it. Five Fire Planets including Aries Sun and a Leo Stellium. What do you think?*

S - What, predict her disease?

N - Yes. Sadly it eventually killed her. A clue: Mars and Jupiter. Gale was an astrologer, too and a good friend. I think we already looked at her chart for Fire. She is no doubt watching me now and laughing. She developed kidney and liver cancer.

S - I was just going to say kidney cancer.

N - I knew that. OK, let's look at the conflict in her chart a la Richard, what do you see.

S - Only one Planet in a Transpersonal Sign, Venus (kidneys?) It's square Saturn.

N - Yes good. I do like Saturn though not in this case.

S - Only one Earth Planet: Mercury in Taurus, ruler of the 12th. Mercury square Pluto, quincunx Neptune.

N - Mars in Water Cancer, it is strongly placed and an emphasis on Fire. Venus is poorly aspected and Saturn is in the 12th. So we have a lot of energy, mostly Fire. It is not being directed though. Mars in Cancer is a poor placement for focus and directing his energy. It is too watery for Mars so she becomes easily frustrated and turns it inwards. Her cancer started in the kidneys then went to the liver.

Amanda: *sex gland cysts which make fluid. She had a lot of problems and so we look for conflict in the Planets first. We would look for Moon, the female sex organs; Pluto, sex organs and reproduction; maybe Neptune for fluids; but mostly Moon for lymph flow.*

S - Moon square Mercury, Mercury ruling her Gemini Ascendant and from the 12th. Also Pluto opposite Jupiter. Pluto is an Earth singleton.

N - Plus there is singleton Moon.

S - Moon singleton how?

N - Its only aspect is with Mercury. This makes it a bit lopsided and it acts less than optimally.

S - Ah, so it just makes the one aspect, OK.

N - Mercury doesn't express very well as its only aspect is a Square. This is not easy to for her to deal with. I would almost add a Chiron Conjunction to the Moon, too. I just might do that anyway.

S - A bit wide for me but conjunct Jupiter means it is also opposite Pluto. Chiron-Pluto is a bad combo.

N - Yes. Chiron is not nicely aspected. Can I tell you something about her childhood?

S - Must have been traumatic.

N - Yes. Hint: Sun in the 12th and the focal point of a T-Square with Jupiter - Chiron - Pluto. Her father abused her.

S - Yes, I can see that now.

N - We have weakness with Moon > feminine issues > her mother ignored her cries for help and told her not to tell the police when she was taken to the station by her school principal. This happened several times. Her mother / Moon > betrayal + abandonment as well as sexuality and femininity issues. We add the conflict with her father / Sun plus some Pluto (sexual assault) and Jupiter and Chiron (psychological wound) and we have some very complex stuff happening. We then add more conflict with a Gemini Rising (mental health issues) and Venus in the 1st House and we have femininity issues. This creates excess worry leading to her becoming a psychological mess. After five years of therapy, she is getting it together. Her Moon aspects tell us a lot about her health problems.

Next chart: **Laura.**

S - Moon square Mercury in the 12th: forbidden to speak.

N - Good. It's a tough one.

S - Grand Water Trine: difficult to introspect on her feelings.

N - Yes. Actually that was a good point. Her husband had affairs and it took her 20 years to reflect and accept it.

S - Wow. Those grand Trines can be trouble.

N - Sure are and we don't teach that enough. Stomach: she almost developed ulcers; bladder very weak and almost diseased. Drinks coffee and wine way too much. Natally, we see Moon in Gemini: stomach and worry but it is not too badly aspected. Saturn on the Ascendant: more worry and some depression. Bladder? Mars? Venus? Sun ruling the 12th, conjunct Mars, square Pluto. What do you think?

S - Powerful will, aggression but with Saturn on the Ascendant maybe it's all held in.

N - Yes. I think she is lost in her 12th House and afraid to use her power. Frustration adds to the worry and stress to develop stomach ulcers.

S - Venus on MC: she needs to be nice to everyone.

N - You are sure right there and the bladder equals Venus.

S - Venus square Saturn, too.

N - Good. We see some environmental influences: consumption of too much coffee and wine, initiated by too much Air (worry and denial).

Marlin: we saw him in the Earth lesson (please refer to his chart). 1st House is too loaded: Moon trine Neptune. Self-anesthetizing through consumption (alcohol in this case).

S - Gawd, awful 1st House.

N - Yes. Jupiter, Pluto and Uranus: same result. Too much partying may lead to liver illness and definitely to large intestine issues. Gemini Sun: worries a lot, so he drinks to manage his anxiety; Moon: fluids, stomach and emotional sensitivity leads to more illness. He had some autoimmune illness, not aids but HIV, I think. Might be that 1st House activity showing but triggered by Gemini and Moon and the T-Square to Sun. See how we have to be holistic?

S - I think autoimmune illness may be a Mars blockage. Mars opposite Mercury, the chart ruler.

N - Yes, I would say it contributes, too.

S - Andrew Weil in 'Spontaneous Healing', talks about a case of a man with low platelet and blood counts, a kind of autoimmune disease. It said the patient got himself on the road to recovery by getting angry.

N - He beat up the doctors?

S - Verbally.

N - What I meant was that we need to see each chart holistically. There are many contributing influences in the astrology of healing.

Leah's chart: Chiron in the 1st House; Gemini Ascendant. A tough one. The fundamental wound: she lost her hearing as a child.

S - One of the senses? Ah.

N - Father had syphilis and it manifests as blindness or deafness in the children.

S - That's terrible.

N - Yes. He also pushed her down the stars when she was just a baby. She now wears hearing aids and lip reads. She can 'listen' to conversations across the room. No one is safe.

S - Sheesh.

N - She developed a bad balance problem, vertigo. Her arthritis and vertigo were so bad that she could hardly move out of her bed. When I first saw her she hadn't been out of the House in twelve months. Her vertigo was so bad that she kept falling over and vomiting. What would be in the natal chart to indicate all this? That becomes an enormous task for an astrologer. I can see two T-Squares, they focus on Sun and Chiron.

S - One of them, yes.

N - I would suggest that the Moon is the worst aspected Planet in the chart so it must involve fluids. For balance, we would suggest Mercury? But then again balance could also be Neptune, Venus or the Moon again as the inner ear contains some fluid. You would have to be one of the best astrologers in the world to read this case correctly. There are no focal plants except perhaps Sun, Chiron and Moon.

S - Mercury is not badly aspected but it is in the 29th degree. Venus is one leg of the other T-Square ruling the 12th House.

N - I am not up on critical degrees but Mercury might not be the Planet. I am thinking it is a combination of Planets, Signs, Houses and Elements.

S - The Moon is unaspected except for the quincunx to Pluto.

N - Opposite Chiron, square Sun, Mercury and Neptune.

S - Oh right, square to Sun, yes. Well that shows the parents in action.

N - *Yes. A truly lovely lady and my best success ever. Lots of psychological problems as well as physical. So here we go back to holistic astrology, holistic healing. OK, we have run out of time. Please choose the last chart to look at.*

S - **JR** please.

N - *First: how close is she to you?*

S - She's not close to me at all. She's the daughter of the friend of an acquaintance.

N - *Good. Moon in the 12th conjunct North Node and Chiron. That's not so good as it suggests anxiety and fear especially with her Mother. Mother issues can create sexual, feminine and psychological issues. Sun in Pisces is nicely aspected: father is OK so far. T-Square focused on Sun and Mercury from Uranus, Moon and North Node. Hmm, maybe her father is not involved with her at all and so she sacrifices her father energy of confidence and vitality to keep mother happy and to reduce anxiety. Cancer Ascendant: sensitive, loves mother but fears her. Moon is in the 12th and heavily aspected. I would say, given the symptoms: anorexia. What do you think?*

S - I don't like that Scorpio combo in the 5th.

N - *Pluto, sexual?*

S - Mars in Scorpio is the sole dispositor.

N - *Insecure about sexuality, fears her sexuality?*

S - I was wondering if she might have been abused in some way last summer and the trauma is expressing itself somatically.

N - *Possible. I have studied many, many charts of abused kids and adults and there are astrological patterns we would look for. We could also say that some will get over sexual assault and some won't. It is not always seen in the chart unless it remains an unresolved conflict: a wound. I feel that this girl's problem has more to do with her mother than her father, brother or uncle. If there were a Neptune aspect to Moon, I would say betrayed by mother.*

S - Sun square Uranus suggests distance, yes. She has Moon opposite Uranus: mother is unpredictable.

N - *Yes. As you said before: somatised trauma, perhaps from her mother. Psychological issues for sure. I think she needs counseling even if she doesn't have anorexia.*

S - Maybe she gets sick so her mother will pay attention to her? All unconscious, of course.

N - *Yes and maybe her mother tried to keep father and daughter apart. Maybe mother was jealous of their relationship because father is in a sacrificial position at the focus of her T-Square. This is Freud's classic Oedipal Complex but with the daughter: mother using the daughter to castrate the father. But I am getting ahead of myself here.*

I think it's less of a T-Square and more of a midpoint picture. Uranus = Sun/Moon - a divorce? I don't know the family details.

S - Uranus is sesquiquadrate the Sun-Moon midpoint. Maybe the daughter needs some kind of reassurance from her mother and it is not forthcoming.

N - *For sure! She has issues with her mother. Her Sun is not allowed to express in any other way but to keep Moon and Uranus happy. In other words her Sun's vitality and happiness is stuck keeping the balance between her inner emotional needs (Moon) and outer anxiety / tension (Uranus).*

S - Did I mention that she's a dancer?

N - *I suspect that her mother may have pushed her into it. There is a lot of anxiety here with her Moon conjunct the 12th cusp, which is very nasty to live with. This can open up the 12th House of fears. Thus she is always in a state of fear: fearing that one of her skeletons will drop into consciousness at any time. It is not good to be this anxious on stage. Maybe she gets ill to escape from dancing? And to gain attention, as you said.*

S - She needs attention in any case with the Sun on the MC but what she's missing is some kind of nurturing, maybe someone to talk to her, listen to her (Moon in Gemini).

N - *She needs counseling and to tell mother 'No'.*

S - No physical illness comes to mind? You think it's mainly emotional?

N - *For sure, then it manifests as physical. Moon: feminine issues, ovaries, period pain, breast issues, tenderness with her periods, PMS.*

S - Moon also a Personal Sign singleton.

N - *Yes. She develops stomach issues, anxiety and it all leads to physical illness. Her possible anorexia is a combination of the lot. Some real sexuality and feminine issues which also lead to anorexia - but I could be totally wrong.*

S - I don't think it's anorexia. Most people don't want to eat when they feel nauseous.

N - *What if she were breathing old, powdered lead paint when asleep at night? Stuffs up our astrology detective work! Or taking drugs?*

S - I suggested they check for parasites and toxins. Drugs don't make you nauseous and feverish. It sounds like a virus on the face of it but that doesn't mean there isn't an emotional component as well.

N - *If she just came back from a tropical country and had parasites that made her feverish like malaria.*

S - She just went to Florida. She was there for some two years previously, too. So no, it was in Florida at the dance competition that the symptoms first showed up.

N - *Ah so? Her chart looks very much like an anxiety disorder to me and as a late teenager this is when it may manifests most severely.*

S - Okay. I will pass that along.

N - *I would bet on anxiety as the key here. It might also be something like a virus as you said: glandular fever but they would have tested for this in the hospital. I think that the Moon is the key to her illness. What about Lyme Disease from a tick bite? Be careful as the mother may not like what you have to say.*

S - I won't be talking to her, her friend will. Too bad if she doesn't like it.

N - *Father is OK: Pisces. She is a nice young lady I feel.*

S – The main thing is for someone to acknowledge the daughter's situation.

Chapter 6

Constitutional health - Part 2 - Signs and Houses

The Signs

Aries - head and autonomic processes of the brain, blood pressure and blood, surgery, accidents and injuries, fevers.

Taurus - neck, eating, throat and tonsils, voice, thyroid gland.

Gemini - mental processes, conscious mind, hands, arms, shoulders, lungs, diaphragm, sensory nervous system. Gemini and Mercury, when overly emphasised, can create worry and fear leading to insomnia and mental disturbances.

Cancer - stomach, chest, breasts, alimentary canal, brain and lung membranes.

Leo - heart, spine, back chest.

Virgo - large and small intestines, digestive system, duodenum, spleen and pancreas.

Libra - adrenal glands, skin, lumbar spine, buttocks, kidneys, acid - alkaline balance.

Scorpio - reproductive system, colon, prostate gland, sexual organs, testes, ovaries, elimination system, bladder and immune systems.

Sagittarius - hips, thighs, sciatic nerve, liver.

Capricorn - knees, joints, bones, skeleton, skin, hair, teeth, nails, gall bladder.

Aquarius - calves, ankles, blood circulation.

Pisces - emotional and nervous disorders, fluid retention, lymph system, feet, toes.

Sign Polarity and Healing

Healing sometimes takes place by addressing the polar opposite. Not necessarily a particularly powerful healing approach but one to stimulate your lateral thinking.

Aries / Libra - The excessive Fire of Aries needs the moderation of Libra and the kidneys to maintain the acid / alkaline (electrolyte) balance of the body.

Taurus / Scorpio - Taurus loves food, Scorpio eliminates it, improving elimination may help resolve Taurus indulgence and throat problems.

Gemini / Sagittarius - worrying thoughts can be managed through activity and exercise, *'Idle hands make the devil's work.'*

Cancer / Capricorn - skin complaints and arthritis of joints resolved through proper diet and 'stomach' health (fresh raw fruit and vegetables).

Leo / Aquarius - heart health through proper circulation.

Virgo / Pisces - fluid toxaemia and lymphatic stagnation improved by proper diet and exercise.

The Houses

We again see an overlap with the Signs and the Planets. Health problems are suspected when a House contains a Stellium (4 or more Planets) and the Sign Ruler (the Planet that rules the Sign on the House cusp) is badly aspected. This is also suggested when the Sign Ruler is poorly aspected to Planets that reside in that particular House.

1st House - physical body, head and eyes, can provide a snapshot of the individual's overall health.

2nd House - ears and hearing, neck, jaw, mouth, throat.

3rd House - lungs, hands, arms, shoulders, head / sensory organs.

4th House - breasts, ribs, stomach.

5th House - back, heart.

6th House - specific health problems are suggested by the Sign on the cusp, the cusp ruler and the Planets in the 6th House; intestines and digestion.

7th House - kidneys, lower back.

8th House - reproductive system, sex organs, kundalini, nightmares / night terrors, overheating and night sweats (especially with a strong Pluto).

9th House - thighs, buttocks, hips.

10th House - skin, hair, teeth, skeletal system.

11th House - circulation, electrical system, ankles.

12th House - feet, lymphatic system, dreams and nightmares.

Cheryll

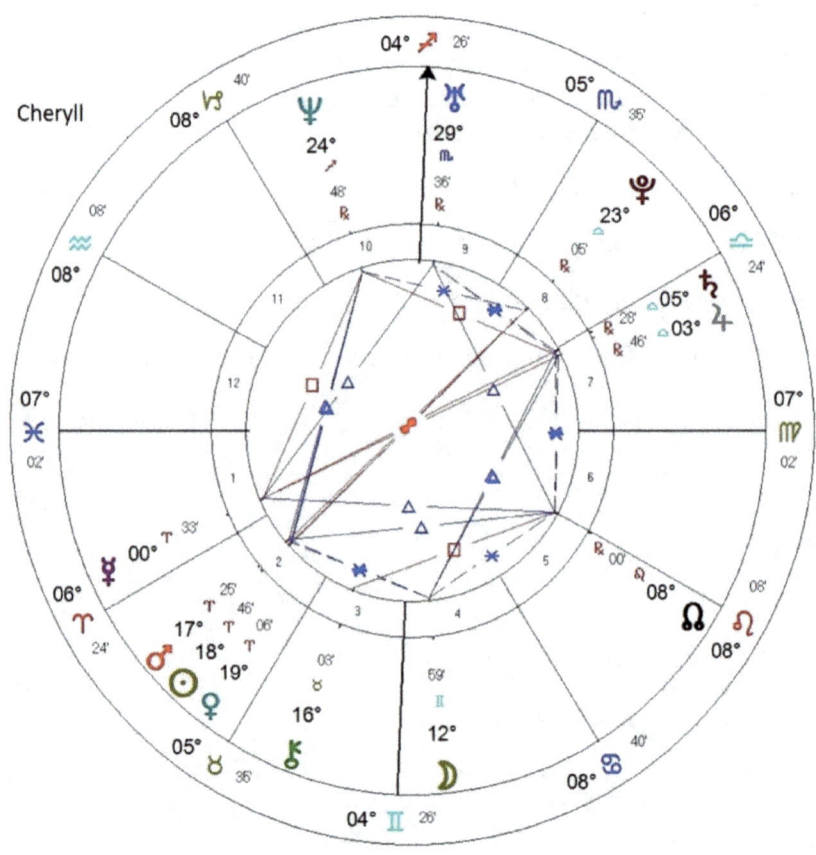

Chart: Cheryll - *look at her Sun conjunct Mars and Venus all opposed by Pluto: father issues but confused. Cheryll's mother was described as somewhat nasty yet her Moon is well aspected, though it is in Gemini: it may suggest that it was difficult to get emotionally close to mother. The Saturn and Jupiter Conjunction in the 7th House contributes to relationship difficulties and it could also indicate that Cheryll feels 'stuck' or trapped in her marriage. You will find out more about Cheryll in the transcripts to this lesson.*

Walter

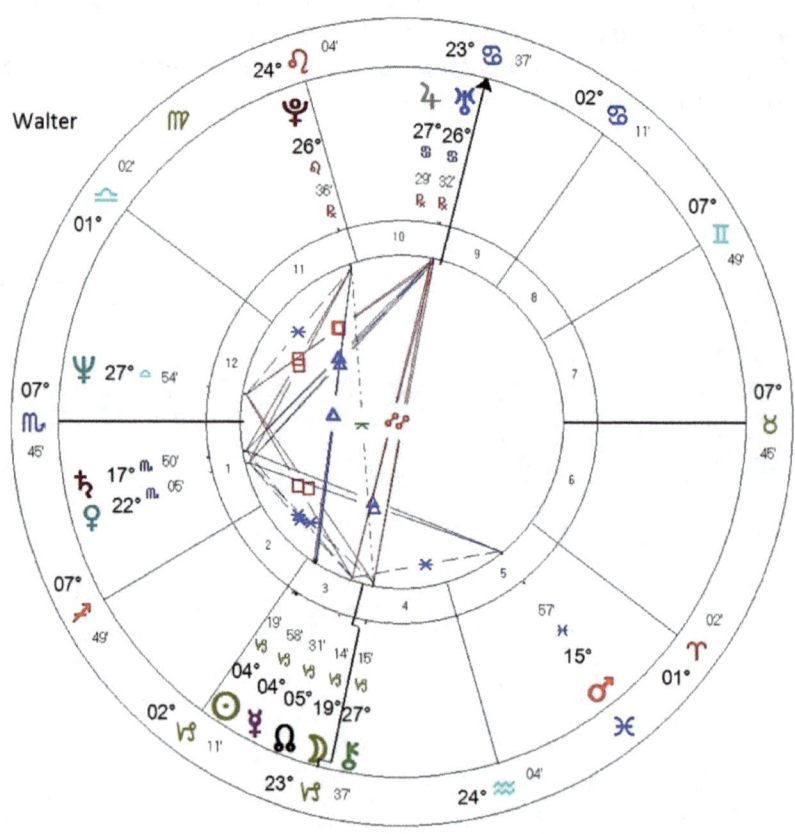

Chart: Walter - *suffered Crohn's disease, and he had marriage problems, the first thing we notice is that he has a very earthy/airy chart. Digging further we see a Water Scorpio Ascendant, a Capricorn Stellium in the airy 3rd House and both Luminaries in Capricorn in the 3rd House.*

Next we see two Planets, Venus and Saturn conjunct in the 1st House, this is important. We could say that this contributes to his marriage problems and makes him irritable in all of his relationships: at work, community, socialising, family, friends and lovers.

Digestive problems arise with his loaded 1st and 3rd Houses, it manifests as incessant worry. Capricorn is stubborn, so his mind will race and it will be difficult to stop once it gets its teeth into a problem; and he won't back down in an argument.

His Neptune is the focal Planet in a T-Square with Moon-Chiron opposite Jupiter-Uranus. We could say that he doesn't deal with his problems well. He tends to avoid them by dissociating (Neptune powerful in the 12th House), running away (Scorpio Ascendant) or denying them (loaded 3rd House).

His Moon is conjunct Chiron and opposed by Jupiter and Uranus—this suggests issues with the stomach and the liver and digestive problems, together with nervousness - all bound together as his primary 'wound' which becomes one of his major life lessons.

There is something important to remember about an Outer Planet (Chiron, Uranus, Jupiter) conjunct or opposite an Inner Planet or a Luminary (Moon): you will learn that the primary health concerns are more visible in the Luminary or the Inner Planet—not so much in the Outer Planet. The Outer Planet affects the Inner Planet it aspects as well as the House it resides, not the other way around.

This is a difficult chart to analyse and it is particularly challenging to determine Walter's health problems, but it can be done, slowly and methodically. There are still many more health issues waiting to be discovered in his chart, it would take us many days to do this properly.

Lesson 6

Student: Fire away when ready.

Noel: *Inner Planets and Outer Planets: just to finish off something I forgot from the last lesson. Astrologers know that the Outer Planets (Saturn, Chiron, Uranus, Neptune and Pluto) strongly influence the Inner Planets (Sun, Moon, Mercury, Venus, Mars and Jupiter). The Outer Planets basically have first say in what happens.*

I am talking about Conjunctions and Oppositions. The Conjunction and Opposition are the most powerful and most visible aspects in the chart and the person's life, therefore their health as well. For example if Venus was conjunct Pluto, Venus becomes highlighted and her negative health qualities now become overly emphasised, as her health is now compromised by Pluto. Her kidneys would be affected by Pluto in some way. It may be in line with sexual activity (Pluto), an imbalance of hormones from her kidney and hormones at puberty, for instance.

Any Inner Planet, Sun and Moon included, will be influenced this way by the Outer Planet. It indicates an imbalance of their physical and mental health qualities when conjunct an Outer Planet. Furthermore, if the faster moving Inner Planet is applying towards the Outer Planet, it is emphasised even more. If the Inner Planet is separating then it is not quite as bad. Have you learned about applying and separating aspects?

S - Yes. The only thing I'm not sure about is how it works if one or both Planets are retrograde and how it works in that case if they will contact each other or not.

N - *Oh. That's a really hard question to answer. What do you think?*

S - I couldn't say, as I haven't seen it discussed ANYwhere.

N - *Me neither. I suspect that the retrograde Planet is already under functioning but only 'just so' in my understanding. Retrograde makes a Planet underfunction just a small amount. I would say that it is considered 'unresolved' or has unfinished business in relation to its Sign and House. If we have an Inner and an Outer Planet retrograde conjunct, this would mean that they both have unresolved issues and this would apply to health, too.*

Natally, we would say that the functions of those two Planets are somewhat poor and you would need to watch these particular health issues. But don't be too stressed because it will be a minor weakness in most cases. Then you would look at Transits and Progressions: Secondary Directions and Solar Arc to see when they are exact conjunct by Transit. Using Transits we work out which Planet will apply first and then when they do form a Conjunction. You can give dates when these particular weaknesses are most likely to occur.

S - If a Retrograde Planet, say Mercury, is moving backward toward Pluto but will go direct before actually reaching Pluto, is Mercury Retrograde still applying to Pluto?

N - Yes. I would say so but for this discussion I would read it both ways: a Retrograde Planet moving backwards towards another Planet is applying to that Planet. But I would also read it as separating from it as well. I know it's very confusing but that's astrology and that's just me. I try to be adaptable and read things in as many possible ways as I can. Then I compare and contrast and make up my mind.

f Mercury is applying. it is becoming more powerful as it approaches Pluto. It is enhancing their Conjunction. It really is not easy to combine the two because the psychological traits are just as strong if not stronger, than the health traits. I believe that it is psychological first, then physical. But hey I'm a psychologist so maybe my bias shows a little.

We look at retrograde and applying aspects in the context of the Whole chart. That is why becoming a good astrologer is so difficult and why I will read Rx (Retrograde) activity as both applying and separating in some cases but not in all cases. Rx is confusing, I know, but astrology is often unclear and I like to view things from as many angles as possible before I make up my mind. This comes from many years of clinical and astrological practice so it's not just a hunch.

The Signs: they basically match the Planets. Do you want me to go through them all? It's in the notes.

S - No, that's okay, I've got the notes right here.

N - One thing I want to mention is that an emphasis on a specific Sign makes for an imbalance on that Sign's health qualities and psychological and physical health go hand in hand with the Planets, Signs and Houses. For instance too much Gemini leads to worry leading to psychological issues leading to somatisation *into the physical which is congestion in the chest, shoulders, stress-related problems, breathing, asthma, headaches, anxiety, worry and disturbed sleep. Now the question is which comes first, the mental or the physical? What do you think? You know what I think but I am far from perfect.*

S - Some people believe that all illness is emotional, mental and spiritual in origin. Others believe that all illness is strictly physical in origin, it's genetic, environmental, lack of personal health maintenance, etc. I think both clearly play a role. In some illnesses perhaps it is the person's excesses that are to blame. In others, maybe the repressed emotions are more causative. I think you can't make generalizations about this. It's just too complex.

N - *Perfect answer, 100%.*

S - Thanks. I mean take cancer. Some people talk about a cancer "personality". Then you've got biochemists now saying that they can induce cancer in the lab by acidifying the body and that as soon as you realize it the cancer cells die. Well if the biochemists are right what's personality got to do with it?

N - *Absolutely right.*

S - Then there's a cell biologist who says that cancer is caused by parasites plus toxins and that as soon as you kill the parasites, the cancer is dead. Maybe the parasites also react to the pH of the blood so it ties in to the biochemists' theory. Who knows?

N - *You're right, who knows. One day we will know, I am certain of that.*

S - I think where emotion and personality really have a great influence is on how a person relates to their body and the body's needs. Education is also a very important part of that. Remember, I told you about a woman loaded with Earth? Taurus Sun, Virgo Moon. Who died of colon cancer? She was an herbalist and very health conscious. She wrote a book on herbs and immunity but it didn't help her a bit, did it?

B - *Says a lot about the power of the Elements.*

S - I think I agree with that, I'm very weak in Fire.

N - *Yes but you have Pluto for motivation.*

S - Saturn in Sagittarius and Uranus in Leo stuck in the 12th

N - *Leo on the 12th?*

S - Yes.

N - *Virgo on the Ascendant?*

S - Yes

N - *Pluto in the 1st?*

S - In 12th, closely conjunct the Ascendant.

N - *You have a powerful applying aspect from Pluto to your very health conscious Virgo Ascendant. You were born to explore and practice natural healing. What's more, to practice tai chi or other chi healing methods. But Leo on the 12th... what is the House and Sign of your Sun?*

S - Pisces in the 7th.

N - *Your health and vitality is grounded by your partner. If he joins you in your daily exercise then wow, look out body.*

S - My problem is that it's hard for me to stick to a regimen. My husband has no problem with that, his Moon is in Taurus opposite Saturn.

N - *Join him, not easy for Pisces, though as your bed keeps calling you back.*

S - He gets up too early for me.

N - *The **Houses**: again similar to Planets and Signs, however the 1st House is very interesting. Anything conjunct or applying to the Ascendant from the 12th House is strongly emphasised. I think of the 1st House as a mini whole chart. Anything in the 1st has first 'dibs' (i.e. first choice) of the native's psychic energy. For instance Pluto in the 1st can dominate all the other Planets in the chart because he has the most energy by his placement in the 1st House. This is a dynamite House. If Mercury in the 7th wants to talk to people but Pluto in the 1st is uncomfortable then Mercury is basically unable to speak. It would be paralysed by fear. Or, if Venus and Mars are in the 1st House and the person wants a quiet rest but Mars and Venus want to party, then the native has no choice but to get up and party. The Houses directly reflect the drives and instincts of the unconscious forces of the archetypes in action.*

We are driven by Planets in the 1st House more so than any other placement. What do you think of that statement?

S - I think you're probably right. That Pluto of mine is conjunct my Ascendant but it is Rx and by latitude it is actually well above the horizon. I think it's really a 12th House Pluto and I don't really have any 1st House Planets.

N - *I think he is very powerful by its placement from the 12th House applying towards the 1st. This is the most powerful point in the chart. We can also call it a 'mundane' Conjunction.*

S - Not even any of the main asteroids. No 1st House Planets and no Planets in Personal Signs I don't think that helps much in terms of taking care of myself.

N - *Lucky you. I have Chiron conjunct my Ascendant and he is pretty darn demanding.*

S - Ah, healer.

N - *Drawn to heal self and others by my good close friend Chiron. But he is also the 'wounded healer' and so I had to get over a few of my own wounds to qualify for his attention. Having no personal Sign Planets in the 1st House ain't too bad. It makes you more detached and that isn't such a bad thing at times.*

S - I think Chiron shows the wound you cannot heal but where you can heal others.

N - *Chiron shows the 'fundamental wound', what you were born with and also as you said, how to help others. Your big thing -and you have two that I know of - are Pluto conjunct Ascendant and Neptune conjunct Moon. And you want more? They drive you to better yourself and to be dynamic despite barriers. What I know of you so far I would say that you are well down your path already so don't be too impatient, as you are very knowledgeable already. Pluto will make sure you do the right things. And Virgo is a perfectionist and very demanding. So between the two, you are right on course.*

S - From your mouth to God's ears.

N - **Houses:** *let's now look at some charts:* **Walter**.

S - Yes I think we haven't done him before.

N - *Let's combine all three: Planets, Sign and Houses and first off we look for conflict.*

S He had Crohn's disease right?

N - *Yes.*

S - He's loaded with Earth through a Capricorn Stellium.

N - *Blockages at the conjunction between gall bladder, pancreas and stomach.*

S - Yikes.

N - *Two things to consider: Earth and the 3rd House. Earth is digestion and elimination and 3rd House is worry. We can see ulceration of the duodenum from worry (Stellium in his 3rd Air House) and the site of injury is Earth (colon). Notice that Capricorn, which is bones and thighs, is not involved in his complaint. In other words he complained about his stomach but nothing else.*

S - It's the Sign opposite Cancer taking the hit. I mean Cancer is opposite Capricorn?

N - *Yes, you are very good. Yes, and it is his wife. We see his Moon is conjunct Chiron opposite Jupiter and Uranus.*

S - Right.

N - *Both square Neptune in the 12th in a T-Square. Part of his issues are mother and wife. The other part is spiritual: his beliefs in the afterlife. But he develops Crohn's disease instead of dealing with his mother and wife issues. I would look at the Significators for worry and the Element Earth to start with, which are the 3rd House and the Earth Element. They stand out as major conflicts. Then as secondary issues his psychological, spiritual issues and relationship issues are sitting behind and driving his physical issues. Any comments?*

S - Mercury in the 3rd is a kind of mentally obsessive placement by itself.

N - *Yes and he is a busy businessman.*

S - His chart ruler Mars is well aspected.

N - *There is one placement that you have to ask me about.*

S - Venus ruling the 12th is conjunct Saturn and square Pluto: that looks nasty to me.

N - *So what does it say?*

S - Especially since Venus is in Scorpio. Well there's an intensity of desire there but repressed apparently by Saturn and all that Capricorn and it shows up as a chronic illness (that's the 12th).

N - *Good. With 12th House Libra. I'll take a guess myself because this is not easy and he does have a complicated chart. Is the nicely placed Venus conjunct Saturn in the 1st House overlooked because of his 3rd House Capricorn Stellium and T-Square? Does this mean that his love interests go on the back burner? Does he deny his airy 3rd House? Because they nicely trine Mars and it sextiles his Stellium. There is little stress placed on them. But Venus conjunct Saturn is traditionally a tough placement for relationships. Does Venus then transform into 'friends' instead of 'lovers' and thus he displaces his Saturn inhibitions onto his friends and by having few intimate friends?*

Perhaps he uses Moon conjunct Chiron to off-set his wife issues instead of Venus. Anyway it is tough to work out, isn't it. By the way, he was also having marriage problems at the time I was treating him.

S - It is difficult. Another chart? **Baby Barbara**? Then **Cheryll**, she's very interesting

N - *Sure.* **Baby Barbara** *is a baby who had high temperatures and fever fits. She was taken to hospital where they stuck a needle into her bladder in front of her mum and dad. They freaked out and fought with the staff and brought her home.*

S - Oof.

N - *They brought her to see me because I was working with them both in clinical hypnotherapy and had small children of my own. I looked at Baby Barbara's chart and noticed how the Fire Element was strong in her chart. Fire chart: Sun and Moon in Leo and 5th House, Fire Aries Ascendant. So she has an emphasis on Fire which can manifest as high temperatures, fevers and when the head gets overheated, as fever fits. The hospital doctor said it might be a kidney infection. In her chart I saw high temperatures, which could bring on fever fits. A kidney inflammation can also cause excessive high temperatures and that can bring on fever fits in small children and even in adults.*

I suggested that mum and dad cut out cow's milk which is a common inflammatory in children. Did you know that the health department recommended no child under the age of 9 months be given cow's milk as it causes bleeding in the bowels? Cow's milk can cause excessive inflammation. Baby Barbara needs plenty of water to cool her Aries and excess Fire. Drink lots of water and play in water: a bath or pool in the heat of the day to stay cool. They also gave her belladonna homeopatically and FerPhos biochemic salts and increased her fresh raw fruits. It worked. In hot weather, she plays in the bath. It was very hot when she was taken to hospital in the first place.

S - My turn to say wow!

N - *We know that excessive Fire can bring about kidney problems but I don't think that it was the actual cause this time, otherwise we would have Libra and Venus conflicted, too. By differentiating between Fire and Venus / Libra they found a suitable preventive approach.*

S - Ah now that's something! To see how the kidney would be affected but to know that the problem starts elsewhere.

N - *I can see in the chart that Mars is in Libra, so there might be a kidney weakness later in life if she does not consume enough water or drinks too much coffee or alcohol.*

S - Mars-Chiron in Libra opposite Saturn.

N - *I didn't think of that at the time, just the immediate reaction of Fire and the signifiers for kidney were not in poor aspect. That, plus knowing that a child's developing immune system was way too young to be fully formed and needed support.*

S - Isn't that bad for the kidney or do you in fact focus on the Planets first and Signs second?

N - *Hmm, I seek conflict first, then the Planets and then where they reside. The Houses, the Elements, then Signs and the last are the Planetary aspects. Stelliums and Conjunctions are always the most powerful aspects. But the Elements give me so much information way and above everything else at first glance.*

S - A Stellium isn't conflict though, it's an imbalance.

N - *Yes.*

S - Hard aspects are conflict.

N - *A Stellium is usually made up of Conjunctions, which can be stressful and Stelliums are very hard to delineate anyway. For me, I look at where it is, such as on an angle. Conflict is found in lots of places but I will say 'imbalance'.* **Baby Barbara's** *Saturn in the 1st. What does that say?*

S - Pressure in the head? Headache?

N - *Yes, inhibition?*

S - Yes and it is hard to express all that Fire energy with Saturn in Aries in the 1st House.

N - *Yes.*

S - It backs up on her.

N - *Yes it is frustration that inhibits the flow of energy to the kidneys. Mars opposite or Mars conjunct Chiron, as you said, is kidneys and adrenals. The doctor was right and about 15 years early.*

S - That suggests an endocrine problem down the road, I think. Chiron and Saturn to Mars is terrible.

N - *They saw a naturopath and used natural remedies to reduce inflammation. If she were an adult we would advise her to manage her kidneys through diet and other means and to handle her frustrations better. Another chart?*

S - Yes, **Cheryll.**

N - *Anorexia?*

S - Yes I think so. Let me tell you what I understand about anorexia. It's a weird kind of dependency problem. The person feels this dependency but despises themselves for it. They deal with it by exercising control over their body, by depriving it of food. They refuse to need food instead of dealing directly with the dependency issue itself. All sorts of things happen along the way. It's essentially an autonomy / dependency conflict. Now looking at Cheryll's chart there's incredible need for autonomy and self-determination. Four Planets in Aries with Sun closely conjunct

Mars and Pluto opposite. The Moon is not badly aspected but there is NO Water in the chart

N - *Ascendant?*

S - Pisces Rising and its Ruler, Neptune, trines the Aries Sun-Mars. So there is also something yielding in the personality, something that gives in to the other person. Even though the Moon is not badly off and with no Water Planets there is a hunger for connection but it's hard to get a fix on that. Chiron is unaspected in Taurus. Maybe she found it hard to exercise her will externally and so did it internally.

N - *Good yes and it is about being unable to express herself, partly anyway. Yes. Let's look at Saturn conjunct Jupiter opposite Mercury and Chiron in the 3rd.*

S - Saturn conjunct Jupiter, right, restraining the desire to take in.

N - *Yes. Saturn and Jupiter conjunct in Libra says 'unable to go forward'; opposite Mercury says 'unable to tell people what is inside me'. Chiron in the 3rd says she is wounded in speech. One part of the problem is that she is locked into a world of silence - trapped. She can't tell her parents or partner how she feels but she had said that her mother was a sod. Mother always put her down, criticised her. Quite a nasty mother. Her Moon (Mother) is well aspected though.*

Here is a moment for you, something that you can look for when you are practicing astrology. Moon = Mother. Mother is nasty yet her Moon is well aspected. This says that mother is obviously or consciously unpleasant. When the issue is conscious, we can deal with it because we are fully aware of it. This is what Cheryll does, she deals with her mother extremely well. But her father was said to be OK, dominating as a child but OK now. Father = Sun. Sun is conjunct Mars and opposite Pluto which is usually associated with fear of violence. Sun conjunct Venus and Mars opposed by Pluto perhaps is sexual violence? Venus trine Neptune says 'I love my father'. This is an unconscious or covert issue.

*This may indicate that **Cheryll** loves her father but is mixed up, confused and mortally afraid of his violent temper perhaps. She projects her fear and anger onto her mother, as mother is easier to deal with. She refuses to face the deeper underlying issues with her father.*

Here we have a classic case of conscious versus unconscious. When it is conscious, we talk about it: "I hate mum!". But when it is unconscious: "Dad's OK, I love him, sort of", it is not dealt with. It becomes the focal point for internal conflict when it is internalised and unconscious. Unconscious conflict corrupts, damages and breaks us down. Cheryll's issues with anorexia may indicate issues with her father (Sun). Unable to express herself and unable to confront her inner issues, she destroys herself.

Anorexia is what you said earlier. Add to that a degree of helplessness and hopelessness and she feels trapped. She is helpless in a hopeless situation and unable to get out of it. This is a very interesting chart for exactly what I have just said. We have deep unconscious issues which cloud the presenting problem.

S - It's weird that she projects her father issue onto her mother, unless she blames her mother rather than her father because she is safer to blame?

N - *That is the point and I think that is exactly what is going on.*

S - The father is too dangerous.

N - *Yes. Thinking of her father triggers too much trauma to handle consciously. I spoke to her father too. He rang up about her fee and I hadn't done her chart at this time either. He came across as a very domineering, nasty man. My skin crawled as I spoke with him. I knew then that he was probably the cause of his daughter's issues. Sometimes our intuition is right and we don't need astrology.*

Chapter 7

Focusing on the whole chart - heredity, Bach remedies, homeopathy, meditating on astrological archetypes for health

Michel Gauquelin found that successful people had certain Planets applying to the Angles (1st, 4th, 7th, 10th House cusps), particularly to the 1st and 10th House cusps (Ascendant and Midheaven or MC). Astrologers know that the Ascendant and the MC are the most influential or powerful Houses, and that Planets applying to the Angles are more powerful than Planets placed anywhere else in the House.

I consider that the most powerful placement is when a Planet is conjunct and separating from the cusp within 5°, or when it is within 8° applying to the cusp. Gauquelin found that doctors, in particular, had Mars and Saturn placed in 'Gauquelin Sectors' which he considered to be within 15° applying to the 1st and 10th Houses (*Planetary Heredity*, 1988).

If we take an entire set of charts for a family and then examine the Moon, Ascendant, Midheaven (MC) and Sun, we would find similarities throughout many generations. For instance, my family has a dominance of Virgo Sun / Moon and Leo Sun / Ascendant plus a powerfully placed Pluto / 8th House. I already know that my grandchildren will follow a similar theme (my first granddaughter certainly does).

In terms of inherited health problems, we already know that each complex or conflicted Planet or Sign brings its own health problems. Medical science has amply documented the incidence of inherited illnesses that run through families over many generations. We don't need to be Einstein to connect astrology with inherited illness, either.

If your Ruling Planet is Neptune, then you can expect other members of your family to have similar conflicts, perhaps slightly modified. Examples would be Pisces Sun, Moon or Ascendant, Neptune conjunct Ascendant, Moon or Sun, or perhaps a Stellium in the 12th House. These all demonstrate that Neptune / Pisces is a major factor in your health.

Conflict as an indicator of health concerns

Let's look at some real cases from previous lessons

From **Baby Barbara's** natal chart we can see the emphasis on Fire: Aries Ascendant, both Sun and Moon in Leo, five points in Fire Signs. Her first reaction to stress or the environment is to produce heat. Heat creates fevers and fevers can produce fits. Barbara was taken to the local hospital with fever fits when she ran a high temperature from teething (breaking new teeth usually around one year of age). Her parents were in a great panic, they didn't know what to do.

They took her to the emergency room at their local hospital whereupon a nurse held their baby down while the doctor punctured her bladder with a very large and frightening needle. Barbara screamed in pain and shock. Her parents were horrified with the apparent cruel, callous and uncaring behaviour of the doctor and his nurse. The doctor thought that Barbara had a bladder or kidney infection which was why they did the procedure.

Looking at the natal chart we suspect that Barbara was feverish and had fits from too much heat in her heart and head (inflammation). Perhaps it was a kidney infection. With such a strong Fire chart she needed to consume larger amounts of water when hot and when teething, to be kept cool during hot weather, cool baths and air-conditioning. The parents were advised to seek professional health support and baby Barbara remained in the best of health since that horrid episode.

Marlin had major health problems, which we saw in his natal chart. His problems were basically toxaemia associated with stress and a poor diet that contributed to a sluggish large intestine. Looking at Marlin's chart, we see Virgo strongly emphasised with a Virgo Ascendant and Stellium in his 1st House, plus his Moon is conjunct the Ascendant applying from the 12th. There is also Pluto conjunct Uranus and Jupiter in the 1st House emphasising the damage and self-destruction of Pluto, the tension of Uranus and the expansiveness and over-the-top behaviour of Jupiter. Immediately, we see the conflict in his 1st House involving Virgo, Moon, Pluto, Jupiter and Uranus.

The Water Element is the main contributor (Moon plus Pluto in the 1st House) and emphasises a sense of abandonment, which was possibly behind or the driver of his ill health. This, plus a strong Air Element, invited a denial of any emotional problems. Earth, however, has seven points, this tells us immediately that power and control of his elimination system is a major health issue.

Toxaemia can result from the large intestines becoming quite sluggish (possibly Leaky Gut Syndrome) allowing toxins to be passed through its permeable wall into the lymphatic and circulatory systems. This is highlighted by Pluto, the Virgo Stellium and the Moon, they all suggest toxaemia.

The pressure of Jupiter and Uranus in his 1st House make it easy for him to consume enormous amounts of alcohol and adds an Element of escapism into oblivion. This is helped by the self-destruction of Pluto when things become too emotional (Moon and Pluto in the 1st House).

With Marlin, we see an underfunctioning assimilation and elimination system, toxaemia, triggered by emotional stress, poor diet, alcohol and a partying lifestyle. Marlin is now onto fresh, raw fruits and juices and improving dramatically.

Another example is **Gale**, who had a kidney transplant during Chiron and Jupiter Transits to her Cancer Ascendant. A high Fire danger, Aries Sun, four Planets in Leo and Mars (her Sun ruler) applying to her Ascendant. She had a great need for Water to quench the Fires of her frustrated Mars.

We can see that Mars is frustrated, he is in the Water Sign of Cancer and poorly aspected, he needed to be kept cool and refreshed. Kidneys, ruled by Mars in this instance, process urine, they generally require plenty of water. If the kidneys become inflamed they can become infected and eventually, diseased.

At the time of her operation, Jupiter, the master dramatist, was applying to the source of her problems: Mars and the Ascendant. Jupiter had unfinished business with Mars and her Cancer Ascendant. She died after a protracted illness and cancer of the liver, ruled by another Fire Planet, Jupiter. Jupiter, incidentally, is exactly opposite her Mars. A beautiful lady, an astrologer whom I greatly respect. We worked closely together to prepare for that fateful day.

Bach Remedies and Astrology of Health

What a lovely way to combine psychological healing with astrology. Candy Hillenbrand in Vol. 24, No. 4 of the Federation of Australian Astrologers journal (1994) has used Bach remedies for years treating the physical body through the emotions as prescribed by Edward Bach. Candy also has a web site: www.aplaceinspace.net

Here is a summary of Candy's findings—Bach's Twelve Healers:

Aries - Impatiens (impatience / patience)

Taurus - Gentian (doubt / understanding)

Gemini - Cerato (self-distrust / wisdom)

Cancer - Clematis (indifference / gentleness)

Leo - Vervain (over-enthusiasm / tolerance)

Virgo - Centaury (weakness / strength)

Libra - Sceranthus (indecision / steadfastness)

Scorpio - Chicory (possessiveness / selfless love)

Sagittarius - Agrimony (restlessness / inner peace)

Capricorn - Mimulus (fear / courage)

Aquarius - Water Violet (aloofness / joy and sharing)

Pisces - Rock Rose (despair / self-transcendence)

Homoeopathy and Astrology

The following is taken from Christine Conrad's article, *A Homeopathic Approach to Astrology*, in the journal of the Federation of Australian Astrologers Vol. 26, No. 4, (1996). A truly great woman, sadly she passed away last year.

Saturn Transits - use Sepia or Thuya to help move through the stuck Saturnian energy. Lac Humanum and Serotonine for natal Saturn.

Uranus - Phosphorus

Mars - anger, Staphysagria

These few come from Christine's article and case studies, you might wish to follow up with a Homoeopathic Materia Medica purchased from a natural therapies bookshop to correlate psychological / physical traits with the Planets and Signs.

HEALING MEDITATIONS

- using the astrological archetypes in meditation as a means of healing

This is a process I use in my practice, we will use **Marlin's** chart to demonstrate how an astrological archetype healing meditation works.

He began his inner journey by starting with his major archetypes: the Planet Moon and the Sign of Virgo. Marlin was guided into a light trance and directed to contact his Moon, who appeared as a slim matronly / motherly woman. Her appearance illustrated Marlin's childhood and his ability to accept and give nurturing in his life. If his relationship with his mother was poor, which it is, then we could expect the Moon to appear slightly undernourished or slightly uncomfortable. By entering the light trance state each day and talking with and hugging the Moon. he was able to receive and learn about nurturing. Marlin's abandonment issues, depression and moodiness began to slowly resolve.

Virgo is the Earth Sign of service and is very strong in Marlin's chart. It shows that he will 'hold in' his feelings before he trusts himself to show them. With Virgo on the Ascendant and with four Planets in Virgo. she is very important. Marlin contacted her to seek a deeper understanding of her role in his life and how she could help him feel more relaxed with others. She has the power to show Marlin how to stop being a servant to everyone and how to gain self-esteem and control in his life.

These two archetypes were just the beginning for his inner healing. By going within his psyche, he can contact his primary sources of power. In Jungian terms, this is the only way to heal, from within. In my experience as a therapist, I believe that this is the best and most powerful method of healing available.

Guest chart—Tania

Tania is a mature-age divorcee with two children and she has been having some bizarre physical ailments over the last few years, starting with an acrimonious divorce. Her chart was provided by one of my students. She specifically requested my support for her health problems, so we worked on it together.

When asked about her emotional state, she said, *"I seem hyper-sensitive to the goings-on in the world. I cry a lot for others' losses. I am overly compassionate, disgruntled and unable to detach. Constantly worried about financial situation, car breaking down, etc. My significant other lives with me and has had a seriously volatile work-life since I've known him. I have been feeling as if I am the financial cohesive agent to my family and I'm sure this is causing me stress as well."*

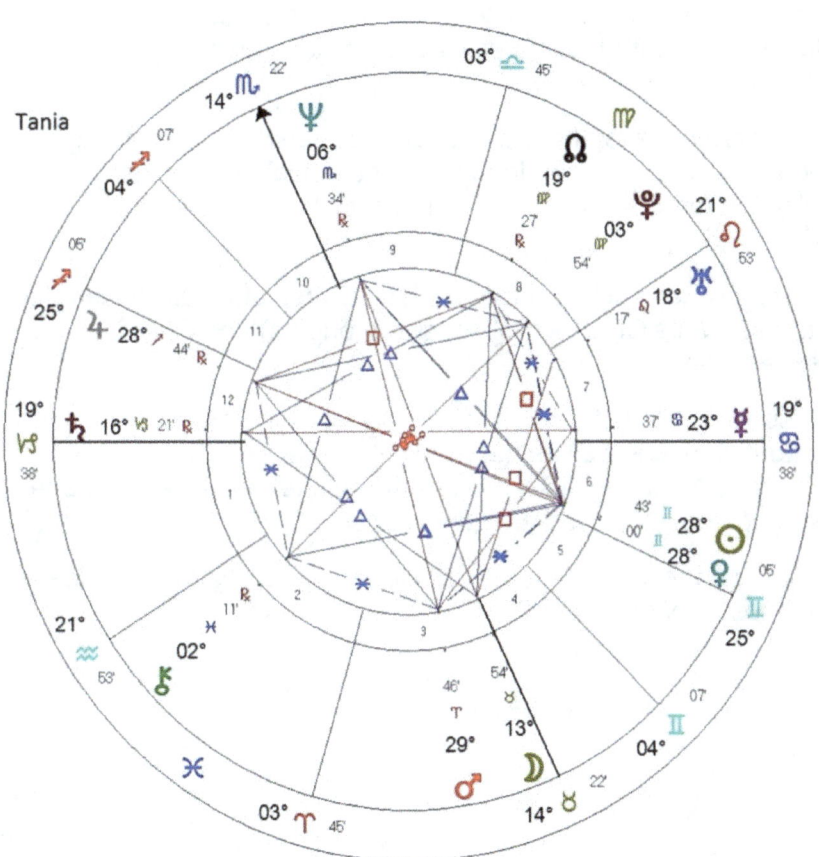

Her doctor recently put her on anti-depressant medication for her worrisome thoughts and weepiness and also an aspirin a day, I guess to prevent her developing clots.

She added: *"History of strong psychic ability, lucid dreaming, pre-cognition, etc. OBE have become frequent this past year."* She asked for: *"any suggestions for a specific healing."*

Looking at her chart, what stands out is Saturn conjunct her Capricorn Ascendant, Moon in Taurus conjunct the 4th House cusp (on an Angle), the Sun / Venus-Jupiter Opposition along the 6th-12th axis in the last degrees of Gemini and Sagittarius -plus a triple Grand Trine.

Not only did transiting Saturn conjoin her natal Sun-Venus but her Solar Arc Uranus was exactly T-Square her natal Opposition. Some suggestions were:

1) Get Dr. Weil's book: '*8 weeks to Optimum Health*' and follow the program he outlines - this was to help her manage her Earth dominance (Saturn conjunct Capricorn Ascendant and Taurus Moon).

2) Limit her intake of news to spare her nerves for her strong Gemini which has a tendency towards denial and avoidance (Moon in the 3rd House and Sun conjunct Venus in Gemini in the 6th).

3) Try the Bach flower remedies Red Chestnut (over-concern for others), White Chestnut (obsessive thoughts) and Oak (exhaustion).

I also suggested she consider seeing a naturopath or acupuncturist as well as her medical specialist. When asked afterward what she did with this advice, she mentioned that she bought a novel instead of a newspaper.

What in her chart tells you that I already knew that this would be the most likely outcome?

Tania has some interesting features. Three Grand Trines highlight her sensitivity to everything around her. Trines are easy flowing aspects between the Planets, the native does not need to put effort into them. Whatever the Trine is related to becomes easy, no effort required or made, and sometimes it can exhibit as laziness.

Elements: five points in Earth, Moon, Pluto, North Node, Saturn, Capricorn Ascendant— Saturn conjunct her Capricorn Ascendant applying from the 12th House highlights Earth. We will add Sun and Venus in the 6th and Chiron in the 2nd House, both are Earth Houses.

Some strong Oppositions: Moon opposite Neptune: abandonment; Saturn opposite Mercury: fear or difficulty in communicating; Jupiter opposite Sun Venus:this suggest that she feels, "others take love and affection off me". The Chiron—Pluto Opposition is generational and we would look at the Houses and Rulerships to delineate this. It's the Inner Planets and the Luminaries that will be most noticeable in their health, look at them first.

Lots of patterns: two Mystic Rectangles; three Grand Trines; a T-Square. Patterns help the native hold their life together, however it is possible that the excess Trines have weakened her resilience, the Oppositions and the T-Square may help strengthen her will though, so if she can connect with those archetypes, she should be able to move forward.

Lesson 7

Noel: We have **Houses, Signs and Planets to combine** and we need to locate conflicts and focal points, plus we have some charts to look at. First of all, Houses 6, 1 and the psychic Houses (4, 8, 12) are all important to health. Why would that be?

Student: Psychic Houses because emotions are involved with our bodily function and self-care. 1st House is the person as a physical being and 6th is the House of responsibility including health maintenance, um, that's all .

N - *As you know I always look for emotional conflict in the chart and the 4th, 8th and 12th will reflect that. The 1st is like a miniature whole chart as it shows the physical as well as the emotional. The 6th is just as you said, it is our own physical health and how we deal with it personally. A Planet on a cusp is much more powerful than anywhere else in the House. Which brings us up to speed. Now heredity in the chart.*

S - Not sure what you mean by heredity?

N - *What we inherit from our parents is seen in the chart from generation to generation. For example, a natal Neptune is a common theme in the family as per the lesson notes. We use astrology themes in our family studies.*

S - Yes, gotcha.

N - *We would also look at a person's chart for a common theme by comparing it with their children's, their parents, grandparents, uncles and aunts: if we had the time that is. We can use this to find a history of their inherited health. The more we know about this, the easier it is to read their individual health. If dad died of pancreatic cancer and he had Saturn poorly placed and your client, his son, has a similar Saturn placement, we might be able to put two and two together. The same with breast cancer and the Moon. If there is a commonality for daughter and mother, we would advise accordingly. So we need to be aware of the genetic link in both physical health of the family and their chart. It is another way to make our job easier.*

The material on **Baby Barbara, Marlin** and **Gale** was there as follow up for the previous lessons so that you have a bit more background on them for reference. The Bach remedies and homeopathics (and this information is very hard to find) is also for *your reference for later practice. Let's now quickly look at using meditation, too.*

It is possible to connect with your chart in a light meditation: just close your eyes and find the Sun, it is easy. We start with the first image that comes in our imagination. Then if we feel comfortable, we continue to work with him. If not, we reject him and ask him to turn into something more acceptable or come back out of trance and go back in again at a better time.

*The Sun basically represents how we feel about ourselves so if we feel bad about ourselves our Sun might appear depressed and unworthy. The Sun is vitality, purpose and our overall spirituality. This includes our emotional and physical health or well-being. Like **Marlin** in the notes, we could locate our health Planet; combination of Planets; Sign or House rulers and meditate on them. We can ask them for specific help and advice and then ask the **Sun or the Moon**, our major Luminaries, for their opinion. Always talk with these two for a reality check.*

S - What is the health Planet?

N - *The health Planet is a Planet that is identified by the archetypes, Sun or Moon, that is most responsible for maintaining our overall health. We can then go straight to that Planet and seek healing support and advice from them. Let's look at charts and combine conflict, House, Sign and Planet and see what we can come up with.*

S - So this health Planet would be a 6th House Planet or a Planet ruling the cusp of the 6th perhaps?

N - *Not necessarily. In fact that is not very common in meditation work. It could be the 6th cusp ruler or perhaps the Sign on the cusp.*

S - OK.

N - *There are no rules for this side of the chart: the inside. For instance one lady I worked with kept dying of asthma and her archetype for healing was Leo who resided on the 8th cusp, I think. He told her to do breathing meditations that I had taught her earlier.*

S - He who?

N - *He is Leo, the zodiac Sign. She met him in meditation while doing therapy with me.*

S - Oh wow.

N - *Leo said she had to do her chi breathing every day. She said that she was too busy. Leo said: "Then I will wake you up in the middle of the night so you can do it." She told me the next session that he did just what he said he would do. She became scared and stopped all forms of meditation. A pity I thought.*

S - She just should have made the damn time. She could do it in the shower.

N - *She was a dream to work with in trance too. It was very easy for her. She was very Cancerian and sadly frightened of her own shadow. She went to Jesus in trance one time and he told her the reason she almost died from asthma was because her mom and dad were always on the brink of divorce. Whenever they were near that point of divorce she became sick and they had to pull together to bring her back. She was quite pale after that revelation.*

S - Oh boy. So she has an attack when she feels things are coming apart?

N - *Yes, exactly. It had become a habit and she developed asthma whenever she got stressed, she couldn't stop it. Whenever she got anxious she got asthma.*

S - A classic neurosis.

N - *Yes, a psychosomatic thing. It just dropped her. She had small children and she wanted it to stop. But such is life.*

S - How do you stop it?

N - *First of all, they have to want to. Then I would work on issues in childhood in a light trance. I would guide them to rescue little Dana when she was frightened of mom and dad breaking up. Then I would get her to go back as an adult, as she is right now, and nurture that little girl. It is a phenomenally effective method. I would then get her to go back in time and talk to her parents and explain what is happening. I would suggest she use her imagination to help them sort out their marital problems and help them raise their children. She should also focus on helping her own little Dana.*

She could imagine that she lived there, as if she were living in the House as a fairy god mother or a nanny like Mary Poppins. If it doesn't go well or the parents become too nasty, I would get Dana to take her little self at birth and raise her herself. She could imagine that she raises her inner baby self just how a little girl needs to be raised. When her anxiety reduces to a point where she is quite safe, I would take her back to childhood again and resolve the issues. I would guide her back to each traumatic event and rescue and resolve them.

Dana would only go back as an adult. This inner work is mostly done from a third person perspective and we would do what needs to be done to resolve and rescue each event. Then I would advance to working with her astrological archetypes to finetune her healing. It takes time and the client needs to be committed to do their meditations at home each day.

S - Wow! A lot of active imagination in your approach.

N - *Yes, sure is. I do this with many traumatised clients at my clinic. It is a very successful therapy for trauma.*

S - You would take the same approach with someone who has a phobia?

N - *I would work first on strengthening their ego and do this third person only to start with. I would go back and look at emotional issues first and work on resolving them. When I think that they are strong enough to confront the phobia, I would work on the phobia itself. Phobias are tough and need a lot of work. I believe in doing the ground work first. If you jump straight in, it could be counterproductive. Process work, psychotherapy, has to be done slowly and carefully. I was lucky to have been mentored by a great psychotherapist many years ago.*

S - Oh yeah.

N - *Best to approach it slowly and gently, as this suits my Taoist approach. Your lady **Tania**?*

S - Yes.

N - *What stands out the most in her chart? What hits you in the eye?*

S - That 6-12 Opposition.

N - *Hmm, maybe, next guess.*

S - I guess you would note the Moon-Uranus Square? Saturn ruling the Ascendant conjunct Ascendant from the 12th?

N - *Maybe but what about the three Grand Trines? All those lines in the chart show that she is super sensitive and perhaps a little lazy and dependent: 'do it for me'.*

S - I see one loose grand Trine: Mars-Jupiter-Pluto. Maybe my orbs are tighter than yours.

N - *I use 10° between Luminaries and Planets and 10° between the Planets themselves. I use large orbs because I find that it provides far more useful and accurate information on their personality.*

S - You and Liz.

N - *Yes, too many Trines is the same as too much Fire, mutables and sensitivity, laziness. It seems that things would always go her way. Too many Trines suggest too much sensitivity to the point where she is no longer in control of her own life: "Others do things for me so I don't need to put in any effort." When she gets stressed and no one is there to put it right for her, she panics and stresses. Then the weaker Planets you mentioned come into play. We look holistically: first come the Elements; then House placement; then specific Planets. We see too many Trines, so straight away we know that she is always looking for someone to rescue her. Then we look at Saturn conjunct the Ascendant, Moon square Uranus and what else?*

S - Sun conjunct Venus opposite Jupiter in the 12th.

N - *Yes, which might be another key to her neediness, her illness, she has so many. It led me to look at the Trines straight away. I knew that with so many unrelated illnesses and symptoms there had to be a psychological basis. Hers is also spiritual as she seeks meaning in her life. When she can't find it, she feels threatened by life. Life feels unsafe, so she feels abandoned and gets sick. Afraid of life, sick, anxious: 'doctors please rescue me', 'someone please rescue me because I can't rescue myself.'*

This brings us to her Venus conjunct Sun on the 6th cusp which is very powerful, too. Her Sun shows low vitality, weakness, no direction (opposite Jupiter in the 12th) she fears being pushed about and rushed too fast. Jupiter is too fast for her so she fears him. Fear is the 12th cusp placement of Jupiter. Then Venus I suspect indicates thyroid (perhaps Jupiter does, too) and it is also over heated, pushed and over-worked by Jupiter's fears. She burns up too much energy by her thyroid because of her fears. OK your turn. What else is happening? I need to rest my typing fingers.

S - Venus is also out-of-bounds in declination. I was wondering what role that Aries Mars plays in all this. She doesn't strike me as someone who expresses anger easily.

N - *Not sure. What do you think?*

S - Strike me.

N - *Ah ha, look at its Opposition to Neptune: abandoned, out of control. When she feels out of control, does she hit out? Perhaps she does when she is not getting her own way and when she feels threatened by someone else taking control. This appears to be what she wants anyway. Her Moon is applying to her 4th House of family, maybe issues here?*

S - Mars in the 3rd.

N - *So what do you think of her Mars?*

S - It's in the last degree. Richard Idemon called that a "schitzy" sort of placement giving a Neptunian cast to the function of that Planet.

N - *Can you tell me why that could happen?*

S - Because the Planet is about to change Signs and change into something else, it's unsure of itself.

N - *And Mars in the 3rd is communication, argumentative.*

S - Yes.

N - *What about Saturn?*

S - Saturn is strong in Capricorn but retrograde in the 12th trine the Moon, repressed emotion.

N - *You bet, she is depressed.*

S - Happens automatically (the Trine), unconsciously (Saturn in the 12th House) so the energy gets driven inward.

N - *Yes and opposite Mercury says that she is frustrated in her inability to talk it out. But what about her health? What should we look for?*

S - Jupiter ruling the 12th House in the 12th opposing Sun-Venus.

N - *Yes and why?*

S - 6-12 axis connected with illness.

N - *Yes. Liver, thyroid, metabolism, blood, vitality?*

S - Heart.

N - *Yes. This is very important because in my opinion the 12th House cusp is one of our weakest cusps, it can rock our socks off with fear. This can set up all sorts of echoes throughout our physical and psychic body. So, straight away, we see health issues. She is very sensitive, maybe a weak heart, thyroid and liver, which can be devastating enough by themselves. I suspect that just the excess of Trines tells us that whatever illness she has it will be very hard to fix. She needs to be spiritually fixed first.*

S - What's wrong spiritually?

N - *By that I mean that she needs to come to terms with her own self-interests and selfishness, her own biases and attitudes. These may be sabotaging her healing. Then we could work on her liver, blood cleaning, stop her drinking alcohol and some counseling. of course.*

S - She doesn't focus on those because of the strong Saturn and Jupiter placement? I mean what is blocking her from getting in touch with herself?

N - *I suspect that it is her own strong belief system that she must be rescued from, not the reverse. There is also the strong denial of her Air Element. What does she do? Does she work?*

S - Yes.

N - *What is it?*

S - I don't know. She said she feels she is the financial mainstay right now and it stresses her.

N - *Maybe she finds that she is unable to help others because she is so preoccupied with her own illnesses and that her family's* dependence on her feels alien. Maybe her husband did all the accounting and money handling stuff?

S - Maybe. So you think she belongs in a helping profession? Makes some sense.

N - *Maybe she relied on him so much that she didn't know what to do? Panic sets in and she starts to fall apart. "Rescue me. I want him back because I can't cope."*

S - Even without the Trines there is that Moon-Neptune Opposition, Neptune elevated, Moon conjunct IC.

N - *Very good, exactly and what does it mean?*

S - Something parental, Mother was a rescuer or a victim?

N - *Oh, very good.*

S - Mother always rescued her?

N - *Maybe mother was abandoned too? Moon opposite Neptune: abandonment.*

S - Or mother was a victim and she learned that being a victim is how you get to be loved?

N - *You're doing well with this.*

S - I have Moon-Neptune conjunct, so I relate.

N - *This lady is very complex and we would take a full family history.*

S - There is also that close Chiron-Pluto Opposition suggesting trauma in childhood. It probably explains her psychic tendencies.

N - *Yes. Let's look at Chiron and Pluto. They are also involved in the Trines involving the 8th and 2nd Houses. What other aspects will help us to determine childhood abuse? A 4th House connection? I can't find one, can you? Unless Venus on the 6th conjunct Sun: "father loves me I love father". Venus ruler of the 4th: "I love home and family?"*

S - Yes.

N - *It's too positive but then again stranger things have happened. Sexual abuse is hard to find in a chart. I've tried, betrayal, yes, abuse, not easy.*

S - Donna Cunningham talks about Mars-Saturn-Pluto connections.

N - *Moon betrayed me: Moon opposite Neptune perhaps. I will have to look at that one and do my own research. The hard thing is that most people with a tough life have Outer Planet issues not just those who have been sexually abused. The latter is not always the single or only issue. Betrayal is usually bigger than the assault and this is not always shown in the chart as sexual but as abandonment and betrayal. We have to be careful as there is nothing worse than making a statement that isn't correct - especially something as touchy as child abuse.*

S - I relate to that first one!

N - *Which one?*

S - Outer Planet issues.

N - *So do I.*

S - My Moon connects to all three.

N - *That's a tough one all right. Yours is mother mine is father.*

S - "It's always something."

N - *Yes. So what do you think of **Tania**? Her chart and health I mean.*

S - Aside from getting checked out and cared for medically, I'd ask her if and how she expresses anger and other feelings of dissatisfaction. Also about how well she communicates with her Significant Other and her children. I'm not in any position to help her psychologically with the rescue issue. Should I suggest counseling?

N - *Yes, that sure would be a good idea. Is she open to that sort of thing?*

S - We'll find out. I think she is very overwhelmed right now.

N - *Oh yeah.*

S - She's overwhelmed by these weird symptoms and worry about her health, but I can suggest that she needs to deal with the underlying emotional stuff.

N - *Yes, try that but it is tough for people who aren't used to it like us.*

S - She asked for a healing but I'm not a magician.

N - *And why not? You do have Pluto and Neptune to back you up. We have run out of time again and you must be ready for dinner?*

S - Okay when will you give the Astrological Magic class?

N - *I just did.*

S - You can say that again. I have to become a shrink to do this stuff, right?

N - *No, just interested enough to apply it. Even if you get it wrong at first, you will get better. You are better than you think and I mean that.*

S - So what's next on our menu?

N - *Let's see… Transits and Progressions later and putting it all together. I'll have to find some charts for you to work through from beginning to end and that will be fun.*

Chapter 8

Triggers or Indicators of illness through Transit, Direction and Progression

The Outer Planets: Jupiter, Saturn, Chiron, Uranus, Neptune and Pluto will always push us towards actions to resolve our psychological and spiritual problems. Jupiter is also known as the Bridging Planet as he links or 'bridges' the Inner Planet group with the Outer Planet group.

Our psyche always seeks balance and harmony to assist the Outer Planets in whatever they are trying to do through their Transits. Planets Transit (or travel) at set intervals to awaken certain traits, characteristics, skills and processes within us. If we refuse to listen, they knock harder and harder until eventually we act or we become sick.

These predetermined opportunities for change are timed by our Progressions. They are also individually known as Transits, Solar Arc Directions and Secondary Progressions. Each natal House cusp and Planet is a sensitive point in the chart. Whenever a progressing Planet crosses these, by Conjunction, Square, Trine or Opposition its associated qualities are triggered. Generally we will feel uncomfortable and seek to change our situation in some way.

I will call all Planetary movements collectively as 'Progressions' from now on. Progressions, as we know, can sometimes be quite painful and stressful for one reason only: they help us strive towards spiritual harmony and to realise our true spiritual selves. Without the dynamic movement of the Planets, there would be no urge for us to change. We could also say that our health reflects these Progressions.

The Progressions are also opportunities to contemplate our physical health problems. Each Progression, particularly by the Outer Planets, will impact our psychological, spiritual and physical health.

Some interesting things happen when a natal point (Planet or House cusp) is progressed for the first time: it initiates the awakening of the specific qualities and unresolved issues associated with that point. This is also determined and qualified by the traits of the progressed Planet. It presents an opportunity to better understand the nature of our natal Planet by how we react during the Progression.

For instance, a Planet in the 'hidden' 12th House has their qualities well-hidden but when triggered by Progression, we will notice an awakening of their innate qualities. Mercury in the 12th House could indicate the native's inability to communicate clearly with others. When a Planet, for example Mars, progresses across natal Mercury, something will happen that demonstrates an awakening of Mercury's hidden qualities. In this example the native may begin to have dreams of specific actions showing how they could communicate with others. These dreams will be specific to Mercury's 12th House needs.

Transits, in particular, vary in their length of time and their orb. In terms, of health we generally place greater attention on the Outer Planets, Jupiter, Saturn, Chiron, Uranus, Neptune, Pluto and sometimes the North Node.

Orbs

Transit orbs for applying aspects (approaching or moving towards the natal point) generally start to activate effects at around 5°. Tension mounts and grows while the Planet applies to the exact degree. It reaches its peak at exact and releases tension as it separates to about 3° past the natal Planet or point.

Transiting Planets are the most difficult to handle when they are applying towards the exact degree. Once they have moved off the exact degree or separating, they lose power. In some cases this will only last a few degrees before they complete their role and their energy dissipates.

Transits = 5° applying and 3° separating, not a strict rule but a good guide.

Progressions and Directions = 1/2 to 1° applying and 1/2 to 1° separating.

Progressed Charts - Transiting / Solar Arc Directed / Secondary Progressed

Moon - the Secondary Progressed Moon shows the domain and the nature of our current problems, this often includes our personal nurturing issues. It is more an indicator rather than a trigger for health problems. Astrologers use the Secondary Progressed Moon as a guidepost by its House, Sign and aspects to the other Planets.

The Moon by Transit: we look at the Full and New Moon and always seek to avoid surgery and other medical procedures the day before, which is when the Moon approaches the Full or New Moon position. Both Full and New Moon can last 3 to 5 days which may prove to be difficult days particularly for recovery after an operation. The transiting Moon can travel 13° in a single day, so it is extremely fast which is why we generally only consider New and Full Moons.

Sun - by Transit is also fast moving. It only takes a single day to cross a Planet or a House cusp and can indicate heart problems or backache, vitality, sometimes self-esteem and generally it is a pleasant Transit. There may also be father and / or husband issues involved with these fast Transits. By Solar Arc Direction, it can show where the next trend begins or when vitality is lost.

Mercury - this Planet is also a very fast Transit and can cross a point in the natal chart in a single day. However, it often goes Retrograde. Mercury Transits can indicate headaches, worry, children issues, nightmares. It has a slightly more pronounced effect by Solar Arc Direction and Secondary Progression. Retrograde Mercury is blamed for miscommunication, computer problems and missed appointments. These transits last only a day, but it can go retrograde for weeks at a time. During this time, it can irritate a natal Planet, point or House cusp if it sits on that point while stationary. Look at communications, minor sensory irritations, finger and toe annoyances, stress and worry, vivid dreams and other Mercurial traits.

Venus - another fast Transit. Venus rarely retrogrades but when it does it can last for a week or two. Venus health qualities include anything to do with the throat and voice box, viruses, tonsils, relationships, mild flu-like inflammations. Stronger effects, positive and negative, may be seen by Directions and Progression, similar to Sun and Mercury. By Transit, it can also trigger pleasant social interactions. Remember, these Inner Planets are generally short, one-day Transits.

Mars - a slightly slower moving Planet, as it is outside Earth's orbit. It is seen as the Planet most responsible for minor accidents, changes in blood pressure, general surgery, cuts, bruises, fevers, heat related headaches, by Transit and Direction / Progression. Transits to a single point in the chart can last a week or more.

Jupiter - Jupiter is a Bridging Planet and sits between the Inner and Outer Planet groups. Its Transits take longer than the Inner Planets just discussed, as it is much further out from the Sun and beyond Earth's orbit. Jupiter Transit effects are seen in addictions and gambling issues, excess alcohol use, manic episodes and liver problems. Transits can last a month or more. When Jupiter transits key points in my own chart, I become hyperactive and take on massive new projects like building a web site, write a book or three, that sort of thing.

The Outer Planets, also called Generational Planets: in Transit, they can dwell on a single degree for weeks, months and the furthest Planets, Pluto and Neptune, will spend years passing back and forth over a single point. This gives them time to actively transform the qualities of the natal Planet, point or House cusp. They will often cross and re-cross a degree several times during their Transit period. This places considerable pressure on the individual to examine and to then transform the particular qualities of the natal point and the transiting Planet. In terms of Solar Arc Directions and Secondary Progressions, they do not actually trigger events but tend to indicate psychological issues that may arise. I find that the Outer Planets are much more powerful (active) in Transit than in Direction or Progression (passive).

Saturn - can dwell on a single degree for months at a time. Saturn initiates change in structures that are no longer functional, such as bad habits. Saturn is seen in such illnesses as arthritis and any long-term physical illness, fatigue, pancreas and spleen, joint pain and swelling. Depression often occurs during a Saturn Transit. Again, Progressions and Directions generally indicate areas of our life that require restructuring and sometimes can indicate health concerns. Saturn Transits in particular can feel very exhausting and it's very important that we get enough sleep. Depression, as mentioned previously, is a common event in Transits to sensitive points in the natal chart.

Chiron - now known as a Minor Planet, Chiron has very similar actions and approaches as Pluto. Transits can indicate when an illness is likely to occur. The natal wound or constitutional weakness can flare up at this time, often for the first time in the person's life. Psychological disturbances can occur, for example depression and anxiety are quite common. Counseling is often a good option through these Transits. Transits can sometimes last many months to a year. Chiron for some reason can trigger or signal some serious health problems, so please do take his Transits seriously and build your immune system before he reaches any sensitive points in your chart. When Chiron crossed my Ascendant, my thyroid crashed and it took me years to recover. He is one nasty dude.

Uranus - responsible for such issues as circulation, tension and anxiety. He is the electrical or nervous system of the body. Sometimes he can suggest a need to escape and to be free. Relationship temptations (affairs) may occur with Transits to Venus, Sun and / or Moon. Mental health issues can arise. It is rare, of course, but they can be triggered when we are experiencing high levels of stress and mental tension / worry. Sometimes pregnancy issues may develop when transiting sensitive points such as the Moon or Venus. Conception can also occur at this time. Uranus is the only Planet to give a tangible reward after he has finished a Transit. Usually, we find that we have gained materially once he has left orb. Transits can last from many months to a year and it is important to learn relaxation and stress management techniques during these times. I become super active during Uranus Transits. I can do a million tasks at once, I have so much energy. The funny thing is that I don't usually notice it until it is over and I have completed an immense amount of work. I also experience enormous stress too.

Neptune - a complicated Planet, responsible for such issues as a vague loss of energy, sleepiness, dizziness, mystery illnesses. He can also trigger depression with a sense of abandonment, confusion, disillusionment, excessive daydreaming, difficulties focusing and confused or dull thinking. We can often feel tricked and used during his Transits, too. , Influenza, coughs and colds and other (often mysterious) infections are common and the situation will often become clearer after Neptune has left orb and separating. A Neptune Transit frequently leaves us with a sense that we've lost control over the events in our life. It can feel like a period of abandonment. It is also the erosion of what we thought were foundational beliefs, attitudes and values forcing us to change our way of thinking and viewing the world. Difficult Neptune Transits are the time to try and see things more clearly by talking to someone we trust or to seek counseling. Transits can last from months to several years. Neptune is a powerful Planet in my own chart and he erodes my rock-hard beliefs and can make me sick with those mystery flus mentioned above.

Pluto - the destroyer may even provoke sleep afflictions if issues and health concerns are not addressed. Pluto is particularly destructive to those who do not pay attention to his warnings of "Let go". Listen to it and let go of what is not working in your life be it relationships, diet, work, etc. Once Pluto has left orb, there are usually unresolved emotional / psychological scars and issues that require you to continue your healing regime. Pluto is the Planet of transformation and he is responsible for forcing you to change what is counter to your spiritual growth be it job, relationship, health or lifestyle. If it isn't moving you towards spiritual transformation, then he will force you to break it down and to rebuild it. If you fight this process, then that is when you can become very unwell. It is a good idea to seek counseling during this time. Transits can last from months to many years. I live with Pluto every day of my life as he is conjunct my Sun, Venus and Mars and they are all sitting on my 8th House cusp. I am still terrified of his Transits.

Revisiting the Natal Planets how they react when Progressed

Sun—heart and vitality, circulation and blood quality may also be affected- There can be a loss of vitality and libido, depression is possible, particularly when aspected by Saturn, Uranus, Neptune, Pluto or Chiron.

Moon—breasts and stomach, female menstrual cycle and gynaecological problems. The Moon is very sensitive, so always watch for women's health problems as well as emotional issues during Transits and Progressions. Sometimes breast lumps can occur during Inner Planet Transits, as well as the monthly Lunar cycle but these are usually short-lived and disappear soon after the Inner Planet is out of orb. The Moon is perhaps the most sensitive of all our natal Planets.

Mercury—the conscious mind, thyroid, hands and sense organs, as well as lungs and nerves.

Venus—throat, tonsils, snoring, weight gain, kidneys.

Mars—accidents, surgery, fevers and blood, blood pressure, cuts and wounds.

Jupiter—liver, addictions, gambling, eating and drinking binges, blood quality, weight gain.

Saturn—gall bladder, spleen and pancreas, depression, bones and skeletal structure, muscle tone.

Chiron—when transited by Outer Planets. it can awaken the natal or constitutional 'wound': the fundamental wound we are all born with. This could be an awareness that we are different, like the sensitive kid growing up in a tough neighbourhood who realises for the first time that he is different from his tough mates. Look to the ruler of the House where Chiron resides for more information on where and how it may manifest during Transits

Uranus—Generational Planet, when transited by an Inner Planet it will generally trigger the issues of the Natal Inner Planet. For example, if Venus transits natal Uranus, then it could trigger Venus issues in the House of both natal Venus and natal Uranus.

Neptune—Generational Planet, when transited by an Inner Planet, it will generally trigger the Natal Inner Planet issues. For example if Venus transits natal Neptune then it could trigger Venus issues in the House of both natal Venus and natal Neptune.

Pluto—Generational Planet, when transited by an Inner Planet, it will generally trigger the issues of that Planet. For example, if Venus transits natal Pluto, then it could trigger Venus issues in the House of both natal Venus and natal Pluto.

North Node—a most interesting point that shows the destined moment of a Transit. In other words, when the North Node is transited, there is an increase in the native's opportunities to grow spiritually according to the nature of the transiting Planet. The lessons learned at that time are of paramount importance and will hold true for the rest of the Planet's cycle. The down side however is that the native is usually so busy coping with the events occurring at the same time that they don't recognise its importance until 6 to 12 months later. Then they will look back to the time of the Transit and realise how much they had learned back then.

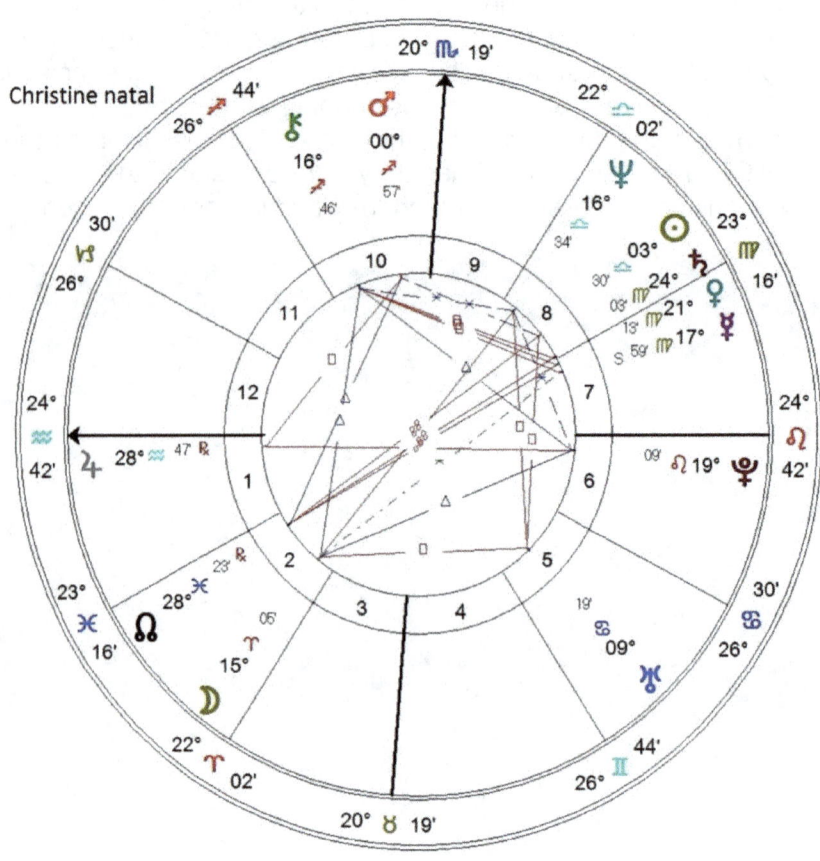

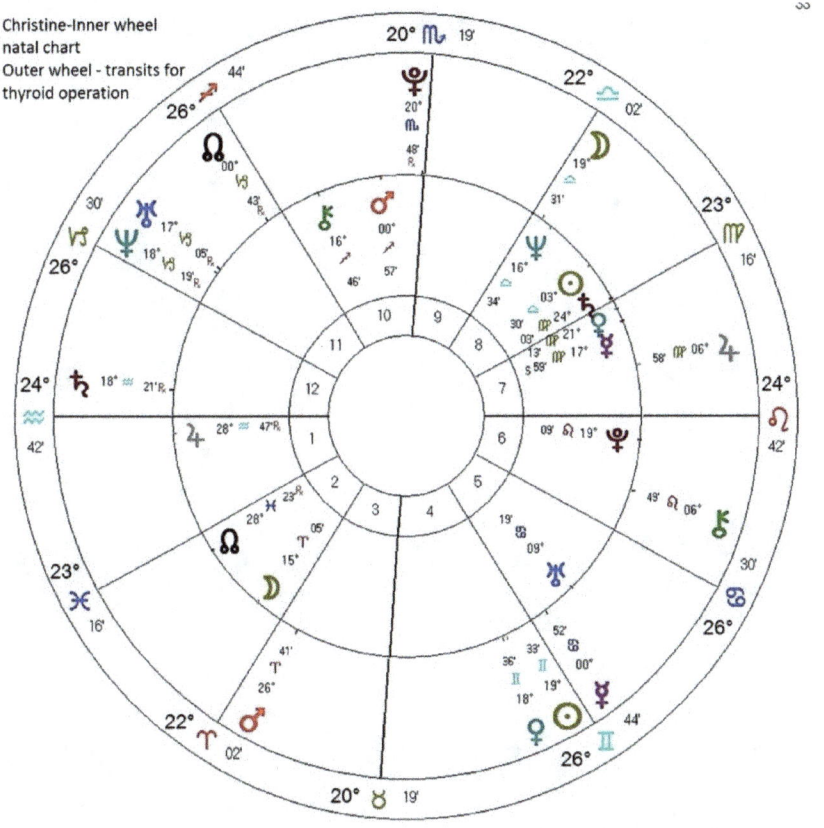

Chart: Christine - *Natal chart Inner Wheel / transiting (Tr) Planets Outer Wheel - thyroid operation. The Transits for her operation include Tr Pluto at the top of the chart, which now becomes her transiting Planet of High Degree. There are also strong Transits from Tr Jupiter, Tr North Node, Tr Chiron yet to occur during her convalescence, which may interfere with her recovery as they are all applying Transits - exactly what we try to avoid during or soon after an operation. This chain of Transits may trigger any unfinished business from the operation and may compromise her rehabilitation.*

Inner Wheel
Christine-natal

Outer Wheel
Christine-Thyroid operation
Sec.Prog. SA in Long

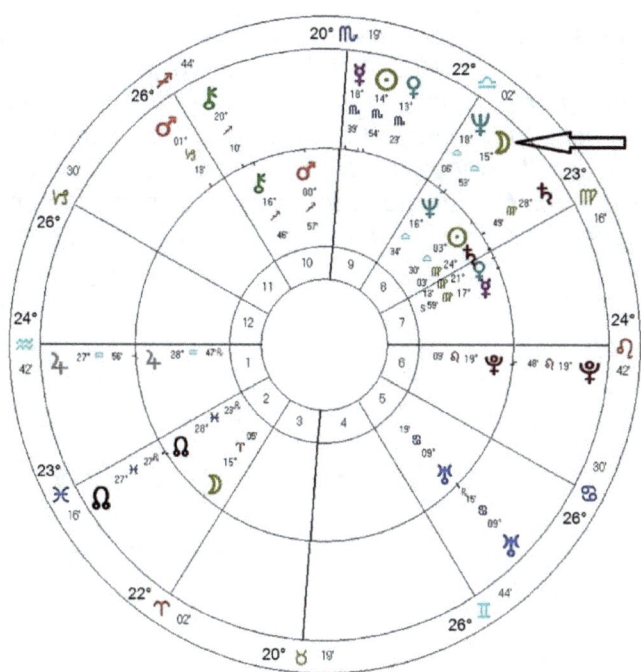

Chart: Christine - *In a Secondary Progressed chart we focus on the Moon, its Sign, House and its Planetary aspects to the Natal Planets and House cusps. Christine's Secondary Progressed Moon is exact opposite her Natal Moon and conjunct her Natal Neptune in the 8th House of transformation through crisis. Full or New Moon and a Conjunction with or an Opposition from Neptune are not good signs for a problem-free operation and recovery.*

Chart: Suzette—*Transits for her operation for female problems. Note on the day of operation and for her the whole period of her recovery, she has to contend with a New Moon (Transiting Moon conjunct Natal Moon); Tr Mars is opposing Na Moon, triggering her 3rd House Stellium (worry); Tr Saturn opposite its Natal Saturn and triggers the Stellium which is opposed by Sun. This would not be a good time to suggest having an operation. As it turned out, she needed several operations after this one to fix the problem.*

Suzette - transits for day of operation

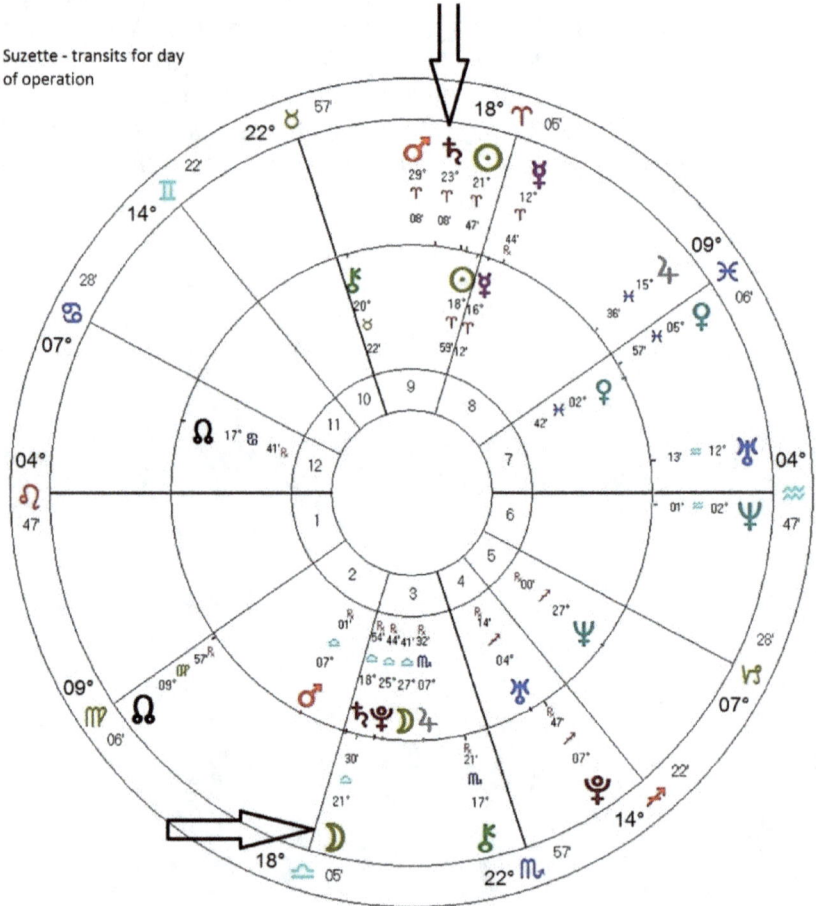

Chart: Suzette - *Secondary Progressed Moon has left its Conjunction with Chiron, so it is just out of orb. However, it suggests that while it was conjunct Chiron there were health concerns—prior to her operation. Secondary Progressed Moon is conjunct and applying to the Midheaven, suggesting that there were issues with her career and she stayed in work to keep promises. This is exactly what happened.*

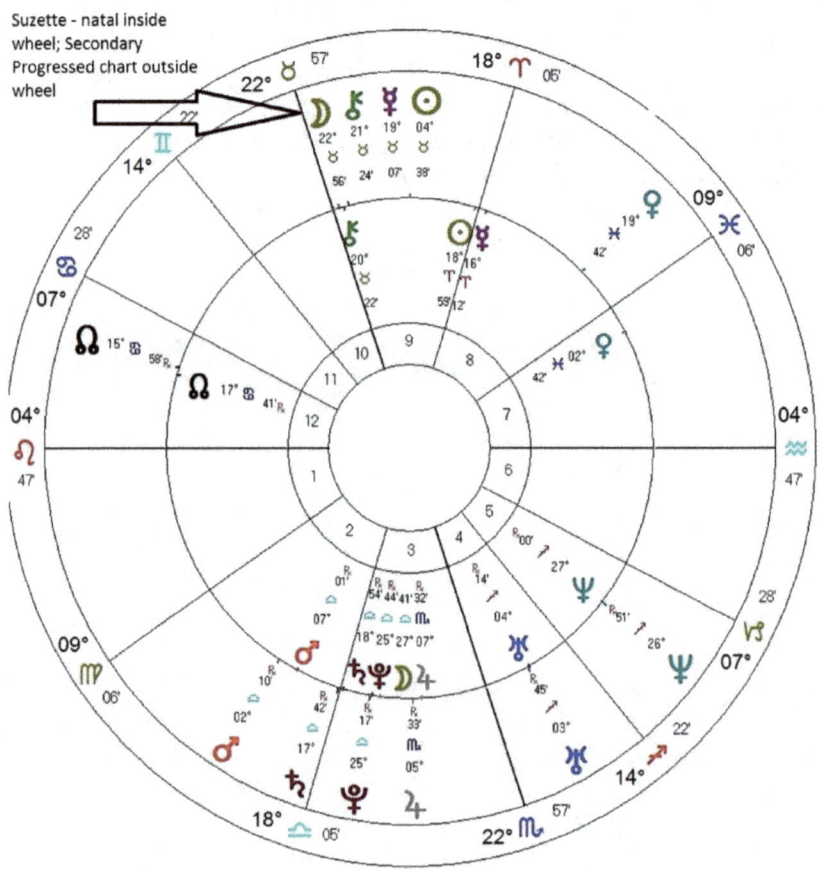

Chart: Suzette—*Solar Arc Directed wheel—viewed as a Wheel rather than a 90° bi dial (next page). We are looking for hard aspects, Squares (90°) from the outside wheel (Solar Arc), to the inside wheel (natal chart)… We keep the orb tight, to within 1/4 to 1 degree. One degree is a year of time, 1/4 a degree is three months.*

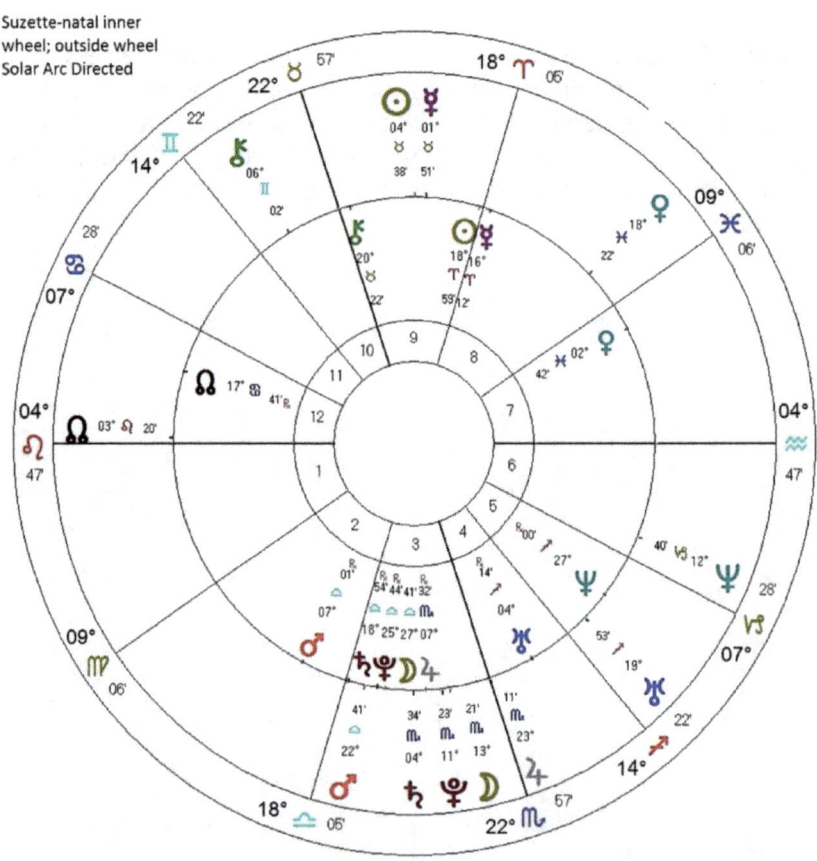

Chart: Suzette—*Solar Arc Directions, 90° bi dial—Operation. We are looking at the Planets in the inner wheel (Natal) to see if they are aligned with an outer wheel Planet (Solar Arc Directed for the day of the operation). It suggests that her psychological state was impacted with some depression, loss of self-esteem, loss of direction in life. It could also suggest that the Solar Arc Sun is acting on the Natal Asc (Ascendant) and Natal Chiron is affected by Solar Arc Asc (Ascendant), Solar Arc Jupiter also has an impact on her Natal Midheaven (there was some loss of vitality for some months afterwards).*

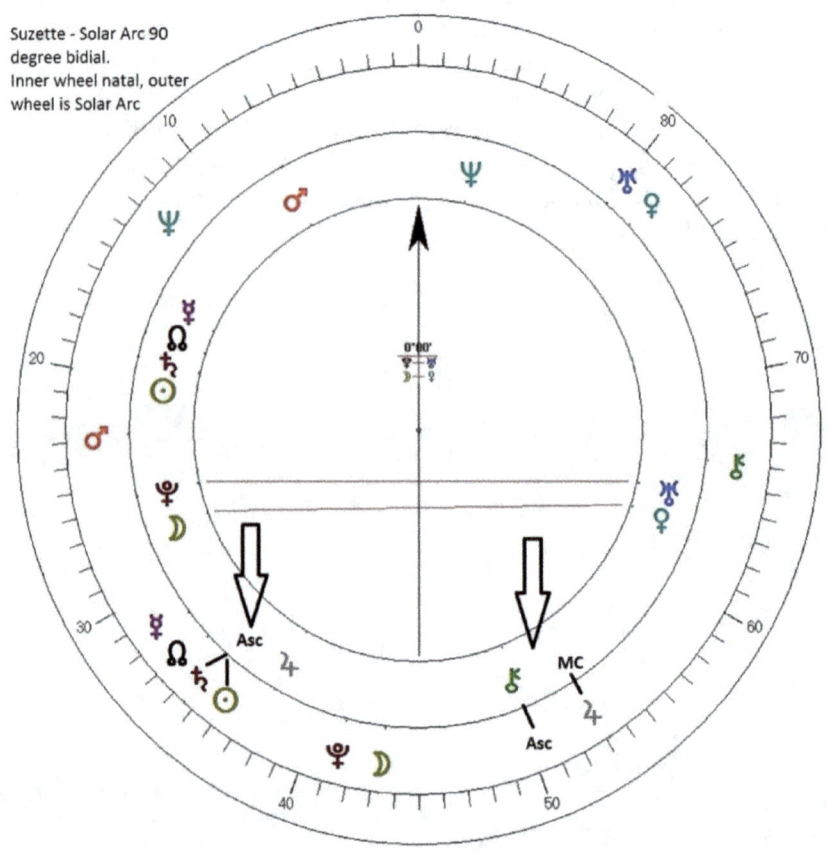

Chart: Lychelle - *natal chart, see discussion in the lesson transcript below.*

Lychelle

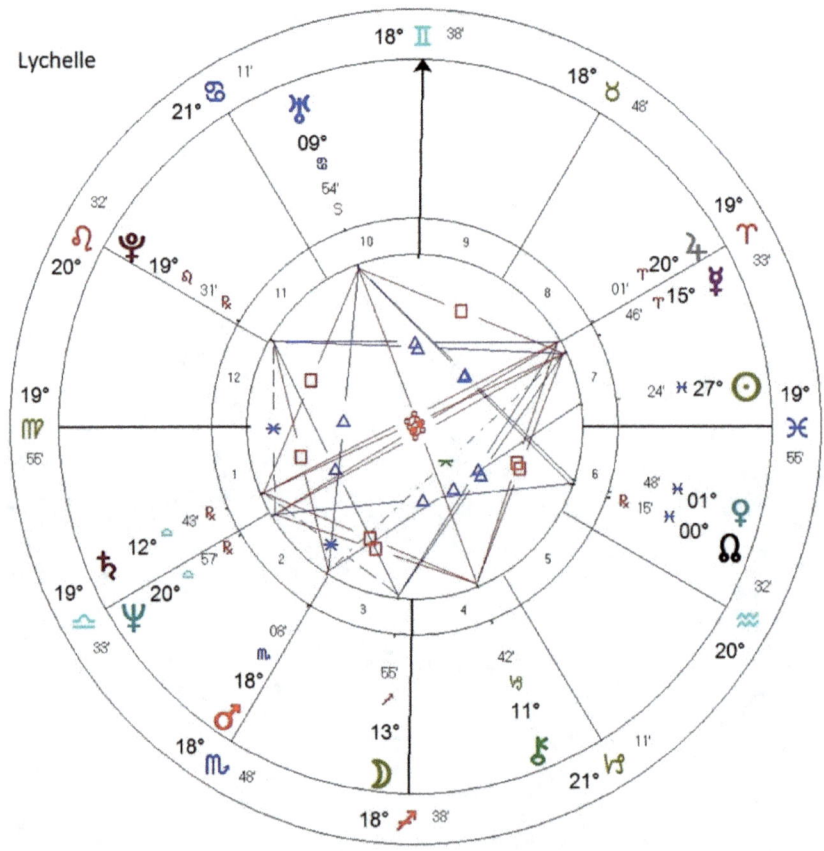

Lesson 8

Noel: *What triggers health problems? It's a big question but astrologers know that it can be seen in the stars. Natal Planets and chart points like the House cusps are the seeds. They can be resting quietly and the awoken by Transit and Progression. Our first set of lessons was all about our natal or constitutional health: what we were born with. But as we have seen, there are many potentials in the natal chart that will never come to fruition unless triggered by some event. We then looked at conflict and what can cause a Planet to make us feel sick and we found that conflicted Planets, Signs, Houses and especially the Elements can combine to make us unwell. But even then it was very hard to locate and decide upon which conflicted Planet, Sign, House or Element was the key indicator. What we have to conclude is that the whole chart is involved, not just single Planets or points. We engage in holistic health astrology, otherwise we can make mistakes and incorrect predictions. We need to look at the whole chart and that includes what is being triggered by which by Transit, Direction or Progression. This makes it a little easier, a little more precise, and we need to be precise in this day of litigation.*

Student: Yes.

N - *Have you thought about insurance?*

S - For medical astrology specifically or just consultation in general?

N - *In general.*

S - I've thought about it, I'm not sure I need it. I'm not giving anyone medical or legal advice.

N - *Just a thought because I have it for my practice now but not when I was practicing only as an astrologer. Think of having a disclaimer of some sort.*

S - A disclaimer is always a good idea. Something like, "I do not claim to be able to predict events precisely." I guess Robert Zoller wouldn't bother with that disclaimer. He believes he can predict events.

N - *The things we need to look at are applying aspects (always applying) make a big poster for this. applying aspects are the most powerful aspects and they can take forever when a Planet goes retrograde. When exact, they burst like a boil or a pimple then as the Planet separates, the tension eases, until they forget all about their problem.*

Orbs can be interesting and again we are holistic and look at the whole chart to see if the natal Planet is already sensitive. If it is sensitive and if it is already poorly aspected, then the orb will be larger. Then we look at the conflict involved with the natal and the transiting Planet.

S - I will volunteer that Bernadette Brady thinks that Saturn Transits have a longer lead time than the other Outer Planets. She says a Saturn Transit begins on the station direct that precedes Saturn's exact aspect to whatever Planet.

N - *I don't quite understand, sorry.*

S - Let's say someone has Venus at 10 Taurus and Saturn goes direct up to 3 Taurus, stations retrograde goes back to 25 Gemini and stations direct and then on the next direct passage will cross 10 Taurus. She'd say the Saturn Transit of Venus begins when Saturn stations at 25 Gemini.

N - *She may be right. As far as my experience suggests, the Transits come into orb and basically initiate the Transit at around 5° of orb. When it goes retrograde it simply eases the issues associated with Venus but it remains tense under the surface. But I may be wrong and it could be exactly as Bernadette Brady says, she is a wonderful astrologer.*

Ready for **Christine***? Let's quickly look at her natal chart first. What do you see natally?*

S - Well there's the Mercury-Venus-Saturn Stellium in Virgo square Chiron. Saturn is the ruler of the 1st and 12th.

N - *Ascendant is Aquarius but I don't normally give Saturn Rulership over Aquarius.*

S - The Transits don't hit that Square.

N - *Which one?*

S - They hit the Cardinal T-cross. Also her MC.

N - *What I see natally of significance is Jupiter conjunct Ascendant. Virgo mini Stellium on the 8th cusp which is important because the Venus and Saturn Conjunction is emotionally involved and if that is not bad enough, it is also conjunct her 8th House cusp.*

S - Yes.

N - *Pluto is strongly placed conjunct Descendant: relationships take a battering here so to make a very quick summary: relationships, relationships and relationships. Add Jupiter conjunct Ascendant and we have addiction to alcohol when relationships fail and Mars focal T Square in the 5th plus Jupiter in the 1st and Air Fire dominance: we have hyperactivity. So Christine is showing a tendency towards an addictive personality and becomes over-enthusiastic with projects. She becomes extremely passionate and hyperactive at times and loves to be in deep and meaningful relationships but fails at them. In fact, she believes that she is a failure in relationships. If we put her emotions / relationships to one side and the addictive Air Fire dominance to the other side, we have the potential for an emotional over-reaction, alcoholism, etc. to any relationship crisis. It is all there in her chart.*

To determine her thyroid illness, we need to look at natal, transiting and Progressed Moon. We see tr Pluto very strong at the top of the chart where he is already sensitive: natally conjunct Descendant. Chiron is transiting the 6th House and then Pluto adds even more to her sensitivity and reactivity. Saturn is showing that he is hibernating in the 12th House and avoids life: he is moving inexorably towards his rebirth into the 1st House. Jupiter will soon cross her Stellium awakening relationship issues and bringing crises, 7th and 8th House, etc.

North Node is soon to transit opposite Sun and Venus and we see relationship issues arising. Venus is only part of her manifestation of physical illness. There were no doubt liver problems to start with, hormonal problems, pancreas under functioning, ovaries affected, sexuality non-existent, low self-esteem and they took out her thyroid which was causing havoc. Oh and her **Secondary Progressed Moon** *shows that it is all a mystery as it is conjunct Neptune. She said that she was in an emotional and physical crisis at the time and her relationship had broken down.*

S - I just noticed that she has a grand Fire Trine. Chiron-Moon-Pluto. That's not too nice.

N - *And this means?*

S - Deep emotional pain and she isn't very good at introspecting and understanding herself because of the Trines. It seems natural to her to be hurt emotionally, physical suffering may be less familiar. I looked at the eclipses that year: Four Solar Eclipses on

14 Capricorn Grand Cross to the Cardinal T-Square. Uranus and Neptune are also conjunct the eclipse. That's a doozy. A solar eclipse with two Outer Planets, POW!

N - *In the 11th House that means?*

S - Square her Moon-Neptune Opposition.

N - *You are doing better than me, again.*

S - It is in the 11th, which suggests a disturbance in her group associations. Not better, just different. The associated lunar eclipse (Dec 1991) squared her nodes. That could be a realization of something wrong in a more personal relationship.

N - *Yes and was it in the 6th House?*

S - No, 29 Gem in the 5th.

N - *Yes of course and the 5th means?*

S - Could be a romantic connection.

N - *Nice, but a Square?*

S - A realization of something wrong.

N - *Why do we focus on the thyroid?*

S - Well the nodes themselves represent "fateful" contacts and connections. The thyroid problem is "presenting the problem". Her endocrine system is under strain because of emotional issues and she probably neglected to maintain her health properly.

N - *Yes you got it exactly. You are a darn good astrologer. I have a feeling from looking at the charts that the thyroid really might not be her main health issue. Moon is aspected by Uranus and Neptune and the eclipse, so her hormones are way out and Jupiter is poorly aspected natally so anything bad just gets worse. Any comments?*

S - Just that the June eclipses and the other Outer Planet Transits that year keep hitting the Cardinal T-Square which includes the Moon.

N - *Ah, yes so it won't go away that easily.*

S - Her Moon is under tremendous pressure. It's the hinge of the Cardinal T-Square and the Grand Fire Trine and it's aspected by all three Outer Planets.

N - *Not Pluto?*

S - Yes trine Pluto.

N - *Separating aspect.*

S - So the eclipses, Uranus, Pluto, and Chiron come along and set off the Moon every which way.

N - *So how would you explain all this to this lady coming for health advice?*

S - I'd talk to her about Moon, Chiron, and Pluto and early childhood trauma. I'd try to pinpoint the date when traumatic stuff happened to her and ask if she could remember anything. Hopefully, she would and I'd explain that emotional trauma experienced at a young age can stay with us into adulthood and create interference, in relationships as well as in our health. If she was open, I'd say she needs to take better care of herself.

N - *What would you suggest?*

S - That there are also underlying issues that she needs to deal with. She needs to eat properly and perhaps take certain supplements that counteract stress.

N - *OK and what about her thyroid, would you have picked that? Would anybody?*

S - She needs to exercise, and develop ways to reduce stress. The thyroid needs iodine but I wouldn't presume to advise her this way. I'd urge her to go see a naturopath. Endocrine imbalance requires professional help. The liver can certainly play a role in that.

N - *That was an extremely well presented comment, perfect advice. OK let's look at* **Suzette**. *What do we see that shows female organ issues? Nataly.*

S - Moon-Pluto conjunct, Moon also ruling 12th of chronic illness.

N - *That enormous Stellium in the 3rd House conjunct Moon includes Pluto and Saturn, so two Outer Planets are heavily impacting Moon and Jupiter expands the negative and positive* influences from these two Outer Planets. This is a difficult Stellium as it is in the House of the conscious mind, worry and stress. If we add Transits and Progressions, what can we see?

S - Mars opposing Moon-Pluto signals surgery for one thing.

N - *And inflammation, with possible bleeding complications and an applying tr Saturn to the Stellium for depression. What about the Secondary Progressed Moon?*

S - Conjunct MC.

N - *Yes and together with Chiron (though it is slightly out of orb), it would have stirred up issues for the previous months and perhaps triggered her decision to have an operation.*

S - Her Secondary Progressed Sun also squares her Ascendant.

N - *Saturn square Ascendant, Jupiter opposite MC, conjunct IC. A lot of Ascendant activity - self-esteem is involved, too.*

S - Solar Arc MC and Chiron trine Mars.

N - *We have seen her natal health issues being triggered by Transit and Solar Arc Progression and Secondary Directions.*

S - Another surgery indicator perhaps.

N - *Yes that is exactly what happened, well picked, she needed follow up surgery. Next chart,* **Lychelle,** *look for feminine things, endometriosis issues. Not much there. Her womb was not healthy.*

S - Here's another Moon in a grand Fire Trine. Is there a pattern here? Maybe the trouble is also connected with the Retrograde (Rx) Uranus in Cancer opposite Chiron. Eww, T-Square to Saturn.

N - *A strong cardinal Grand Cross and a Fire Grand Trine and don't forget that I use larger orbs.*

S - Yes a Grand Cross with Mercury and I didn't forget. Mercury is the hinge there and rules her Ascendant.

N - *Look, Venus and Sun.*

S - Exalted in Pisces but unaspected.

N - *Yes very important. Unaspected means it is not connected to her psyche, so sexuality is disconnected from the norm. She said that she is a lesbian, so perhaps the unaspected Venus contributes to her female organ illness.*

S - Oh that's interesting. I don't think her sexuality is disconnected as she's got a Mars-Pluto Square. How much you want to bet she's butch?

N - *I bet she's tough but not butch with that Venus in Pisces.*

S - It may be repressed and she may let her partner carry that for her.

N - *Well Dr Jung you got me on that one. You may be right.*

S - Doesn't Scorpio rule the organs of reproduction?

N - *Yes, he sure does, partly. Pluto sits where?*

S - Mars in Scorpio is her sole dispositor.

N - *On her 12th cusp.*

S - And it's squared by Pluto.

N - *There may be a fear of sexuality, perhaps something happened? There is a definite focus on Venus / Pluto / Sun which could cause health problems with her sexual organs.*

S - Why? Sun?

N - *Sun is a singleton and has only a single aspect. It only has one outlet through Mars, so because of this he is important to consider. A singleton is always a stand-out Planet to watch out for, I think.*

S - So wouldn't that make sexuality more important?

N - *Yes Sun is self-esteem, belief in oneself and I think it may influence sexual preferences. It may turn push into shove so to speak. The old Golden Rule of astrology: If it is there once = maybe, twice = probably, three times = definitely.*

She has Venus, Sun and Pluto all showing sexuality, sex organs, self-esteem and fear. Put it together and we could find someone who is not sure about who to turn to for comfort and support. Moon is strong, so maybe the butch bit comes out here. OK let's look at her Secondary Progressed chart for an operation.

S - I've got Christiane Northrup's book here, 'Women's Bodies, Women's Wisdom'.

N – *Yes?*

S - She says endometriosis is a disease of [internal] competition.

N- *That is interesting what else does she say?*

S - "It comes about when a woman's emotional needs are competing with her functioning in the outside world."

N - *Shows the conflict internally with the natal Planets, Signs and Elements - yes?*

S - It may be her relating needs (Venus) specifically that she's ignoring.

N - *Ah, yes of course, loss of motherhood perhaps? OK what does the Secondary Progressed chart show?* **(in the next lesson notes)**

S - Secondary Progressed Moon is opposite her Mercury the hinge Planet ruling her Ascendant. Brings the inadequacies in her relating style to the fore, perhaps?

N - *But not much about her operation.*

S - No, what about the Arcs?

N - *Arcs?*

S - Solar Arcs?

N - *Her Solar Arcs show Saturn square Venus as the only aspect other than North Node conjunct Jupiter.*

S - Ah yes, that would bring the internal conflict out, yes. Internal pressure creating illness.

N - *Yes, and shows that this is an important time for her, fated. I forgot to add the transit chart as it shows Pluto conjunct Moon just separating.*

S - You sure did! Oh well! There ya go!

N - *We will use her charts for our next lesson anyway, phew!*

S - She had the operation this year? Her Moon was hit last fall by the first two Saturn-Pluto Oppositions.

N - *Yes, she went through hell plus there was some Chiron influence, too, some time ago. I will post this chart in the next lesson.*

S - So what is it with those Grand Fire Trines anyway?

N - *Increases her sensitivity.*

S - Umm, I can't agree. My mother has one, a double, in fact and she's remarkably insensitive.

N - *Enthusiasm that is squashed can produce disappointment and depression. By sensitivity I mean to outside events which can be internalised to produce health problems. Sensitivity is not compassion and empathy, especially for Fire Signs.*

S - I think the only way you get from a Grand Fire Trine to illness is by way of denial and not even acknowledging that anything is bothering you. It works for my mother.

N - *I think Trines might sometimes weaken the native's resilience in some ways. OK thanks for tonight's chat, see ya next week for our last lesson.*

S - This has really been a blast.

N - *Thanks, but it wasn't an easy lesson.*

S - It's not a cut-and-dried subject that's for sure - but it's very important. I just got Marcia Starck's new book, she's a famous American medical astrologer. She's written a bunch of books and she has a correspondence course in medical astrology. She's also into Earth Medicine. She's director of an organization devoted to helping folks through ancient rituals and modern spiritual practices. I guess astrology falls in the latter category. Not a Wiccan, as far as I know. Anyway, her new book just came out and got good reviews.

Chapter 9

Operations - timing an operation, healing miracles, astrological archetypes in meditation

There are some important points to make about the timing for upcoming operations or medical procedures: health appears to worsen during an applying Transit. Try to seek either no Transits or a separating Transit for an operation or medical procedure. There are so many Transits (Progressions + Directions) occurring that it is really quite hard to find the best time and ill health usually flares up during Transits anyway.

Over the centuries astrologers have made many suggestions about when to have an operation. Most commonly, they advise that it is best to try for a separating Transit if you have the option. In an emergency, please use your common sense and don't hesitate to go to the hospital as soon as possible.

A simple technique is to look at the transiting Moon. Try to time your operation after the Full Moon or after the New Moon: both are separating aspects. Other Planets to look out for are Mars (bleeding and surgery) and Neptune (hidden side-effects, incomplete results, infections and mysterious illnesses).

I always consider Pluto and Chiron Transits as very difficult. Do try for a separating aspect when they are in Transit to the Angles, Luminaries or Inner Planets. The Outer Planets are: Jupiter, Saturn, Chiron, Uranus, Neptune and Pluto. I only consider Outer Planets when they are transited by the Inner Planets or Luminaries. An Outer Planet transiting an Outer Planet, for instance, Saturn square Uranus, is not going to be as powerful as, say, transiting Mercury square Uranus.

A simple rule of thumb is: when the Outer Planets Transit each other, they are not as powerful as when they transit or are transited by an Inner Planet or a Luminary. Yes, they do have influence but then everybody about the same age will have the exact same influence according to their House placement. Stick to the Inner Planets and Luminaries when considering Transits from or to these powerful Outer Planets.

We would be careful with Transits to the Ascendant, Moon and Sun in particular and also with Transits to the 12th and 6th House cusps. Major Transits are the Conjunction (strongest), Opposition (next strongest), followed by the Square and the Trine. I rarely use other aspects such as sextile or quincunx. They do have influence but are not as powerful as the Conjunction and Opposition.

Second rule of thumb: always consider the most powerful transiting aspects first. Conjunction followed by Opposition. Next are the Square and Trine. A minor aspect does not trigger major health problems.

Third rule of thumb: it is best to avoid an applying aspect when you are seeking an operation because an applying aspect indicates that there is going to be some unfinished business afterward. This may affect your recovery, as the Transit will continue after the operation until the Planet separates.

The Moon can prove to be a problem for operations. Both Full and New Moon phases appear to enhance bleeding. Otherwise they are not as serious as the Outer Planet Transits. Scientific findings on the Moon's influence in healing is inconclusive, though it is wise to avoid applying aspects as discussed above.

The basic rule of thumb for this chapter is: try to avoid any applying major Outer Planet Transit. The term we would use for an applying Transit is 'unfinished business'

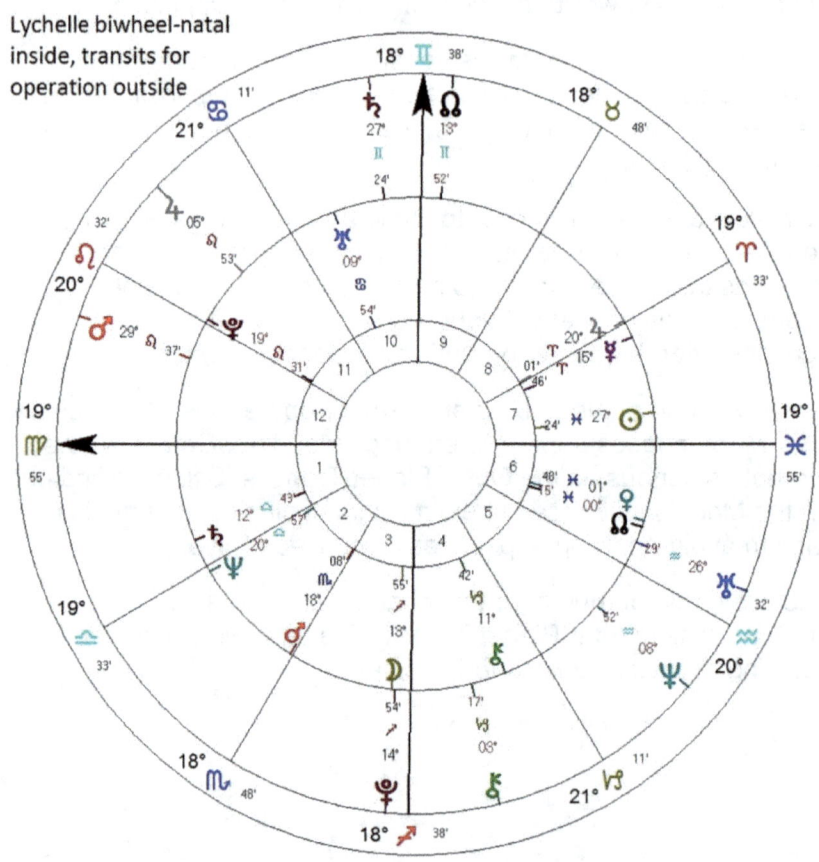

Chart: Lychelle - *we discussed her natal chart briefly in the previous lesson, she had a hysterectomy, endometriosis and ovary problem, they removed her uterus and ovaries. Why is she unwell at this time? What were her illness triggers? The inner wheel is the natal charts, the outer wheel shows Transits for her hysterectomy operation.*

Note: the psychological and physiological impact of transiting Pluto crossing her natal Moon. Fortunately this is a separating aspect, Pluto does not retrograde back to the exact Moon degree. Transiting Venus is also separating from a Conjunction with Neptune, another fortuitous Sign for her operation. North Node is exactly opposite her Natal Moon, suggesting that this is a destined opportunity for Lychelle to make changes in her life. Lychelle knew she was unwell, she went to the best medical specialists available, she booked her operation without any knowledge of medical astrology. Yet it was a perfect time, not one applying aspect and she made a complete recovery.

Nev-inner natal, outer transits operation

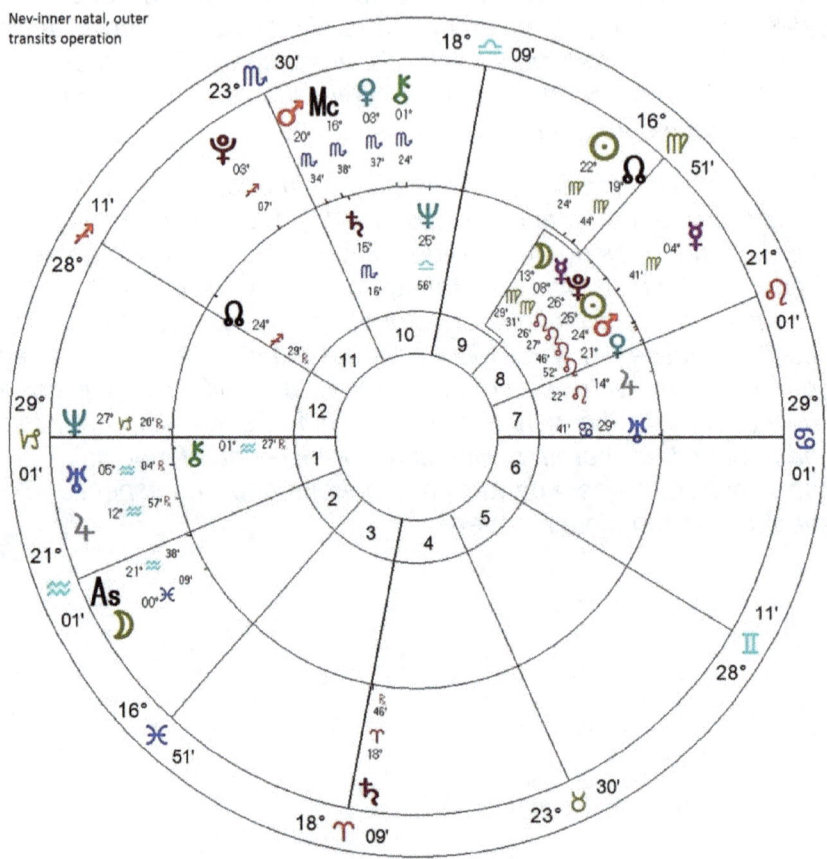

Chart: Nev - A terrible time for an operation. Look at Transiting Neptune about to cross the Ascendant, an applying aspect showing that it was going to fail—and it did. Any transiting Conjunctions to the Moon, Sun or Ascendant, suggest difficulties for an operation. Avoid them if you can, if you can't, then be careful and look after yourself.

Nev - 2nd eye operation - inner wheel natal chart; outer wheel transits

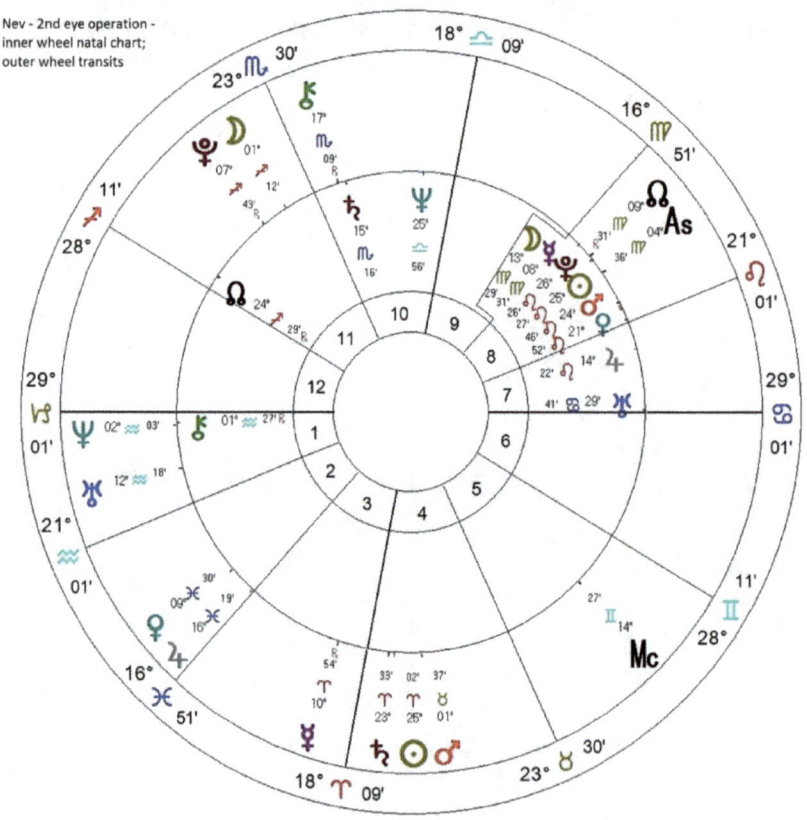

***Chart:* Nev** - *his second operation was a resounding success, Tr Neptune had crossed his Ascendant and he had no other conflicting or negative major Transits. Note Transiting Sun is opposite Natal Neptune, a fast moving Transit, which may have put a little fear into him for the day but not strong enough to do any damage.*

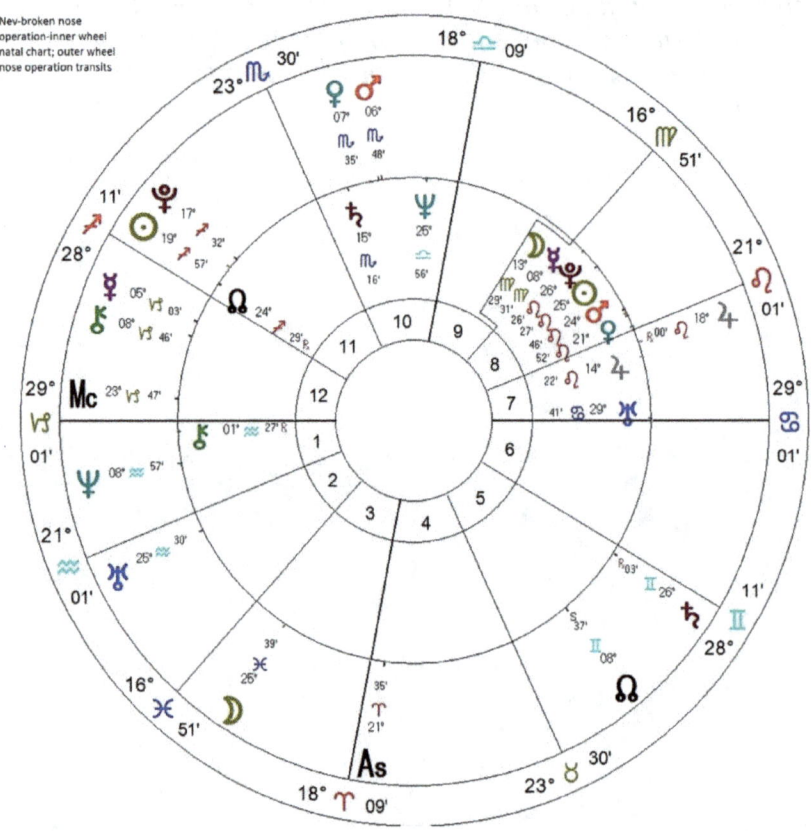

Nev-broken nose operation-inner wheel natal chart; outer wheel nose operation transits

Chart: Nev - *Transits for his broken nose operation. Note that Transiting Uranus opposes his Natal Sun, why wasn't that a problem? Tr Uranus had been crossing his Natal Sun for two years previously and was just on its final pass. It had completed its business, it had nothing more to do.*

A point for you to remember: Outer Planets do most of their transformation (and this can be painful and cause medical problems) during their first few passes over the exact degree of the Natal Planet, their final pass is usually quite uneventful. Transiting Uranus had done what he needed to do with Nev's Sun and was now leaving.

Tara - biwheel of transits for emergency caesarian. Inner wheel natal chart; outerwheel operation/birth

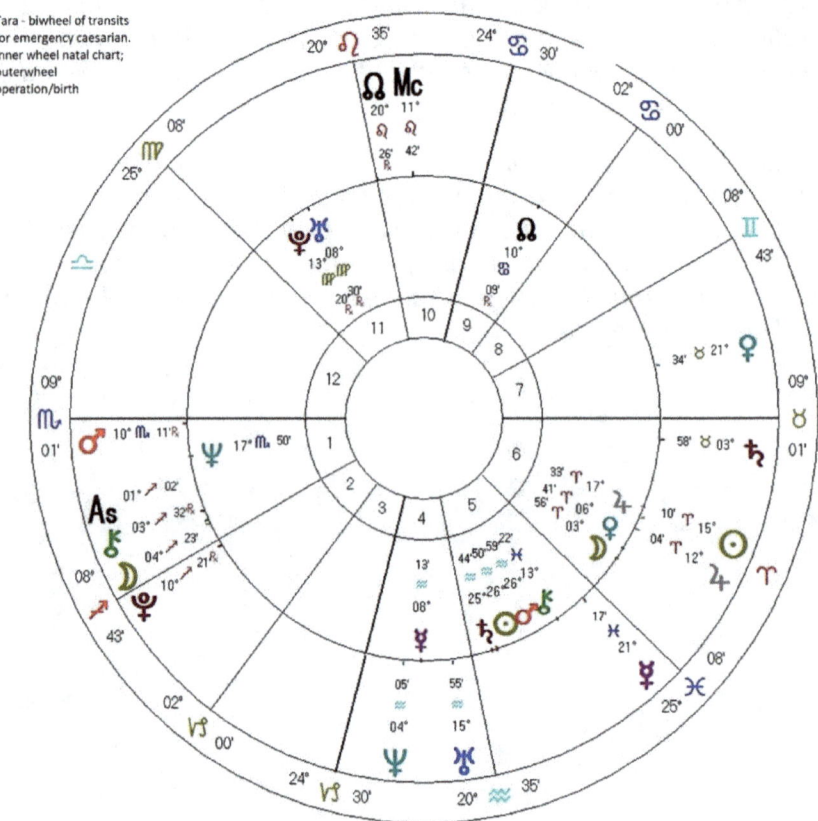

Chart: Tara - *Emergency caesarean—her uterus was damaged, she nearly bled to death during the birth of her daughter. Note the placement of Transiting Mars (Retrograde) just below the Ascendant and retrograding back towards it, thus it became an applying Transit (by retrograde). It became a dreadful day that might have been avoided if the baby arrived earlier.*

Note: Mars didn't go Direct again for two months—I don't think she could have held off that long. I guess that's just life.

Jock - natal

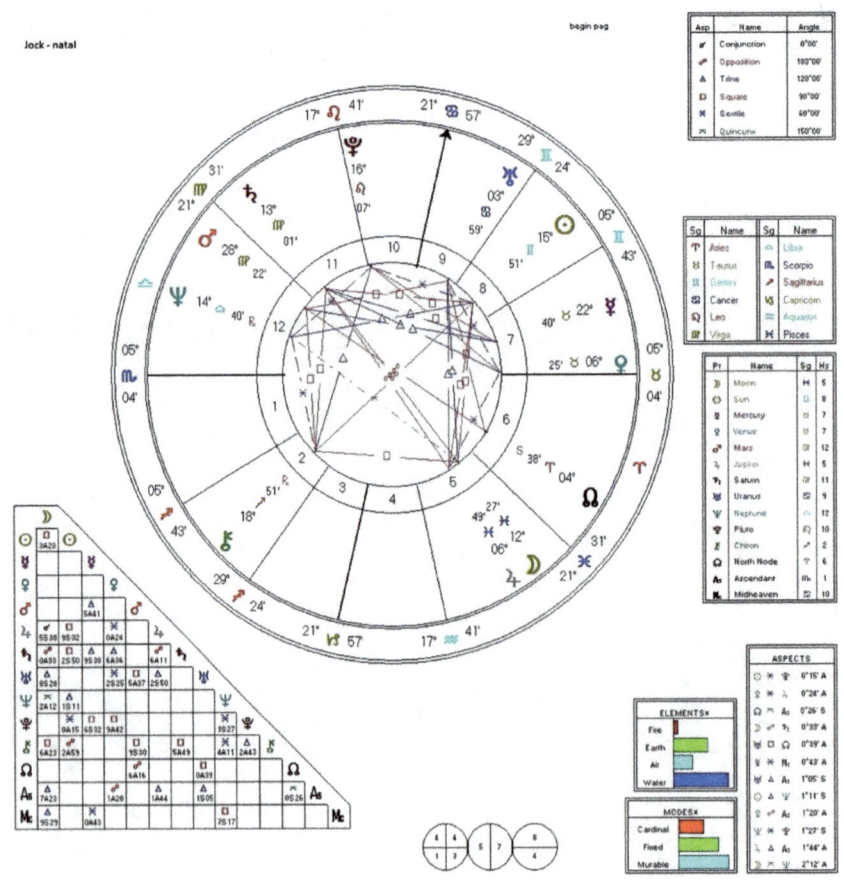

Chart: Jock - *natal - we discuss Jock's operation charts in the following transcripts.*

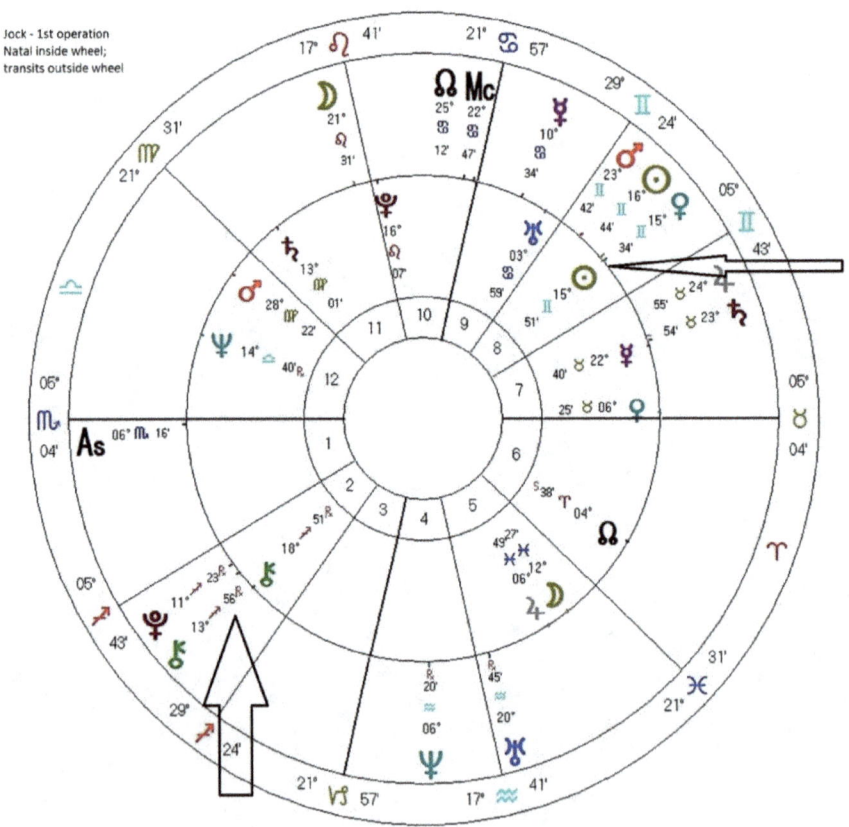

Chart: Jock - *operation, birth chart inside wheel, outside wheel shows his operation for prostate cancer. Why did it come back 2 years later?*

Look at those two applying Transits from the two most powerful Outer Planets: Pluto and Chiron in the 2nd House, opposing his natal Sun. Chiron was also about to have a return to its natal position. These two transiting Planets to his Sun surely suggest unfinished business of the nastiest kind.

Jock - checkup.
Biwheel, natal inside wheel, transits outside wheel

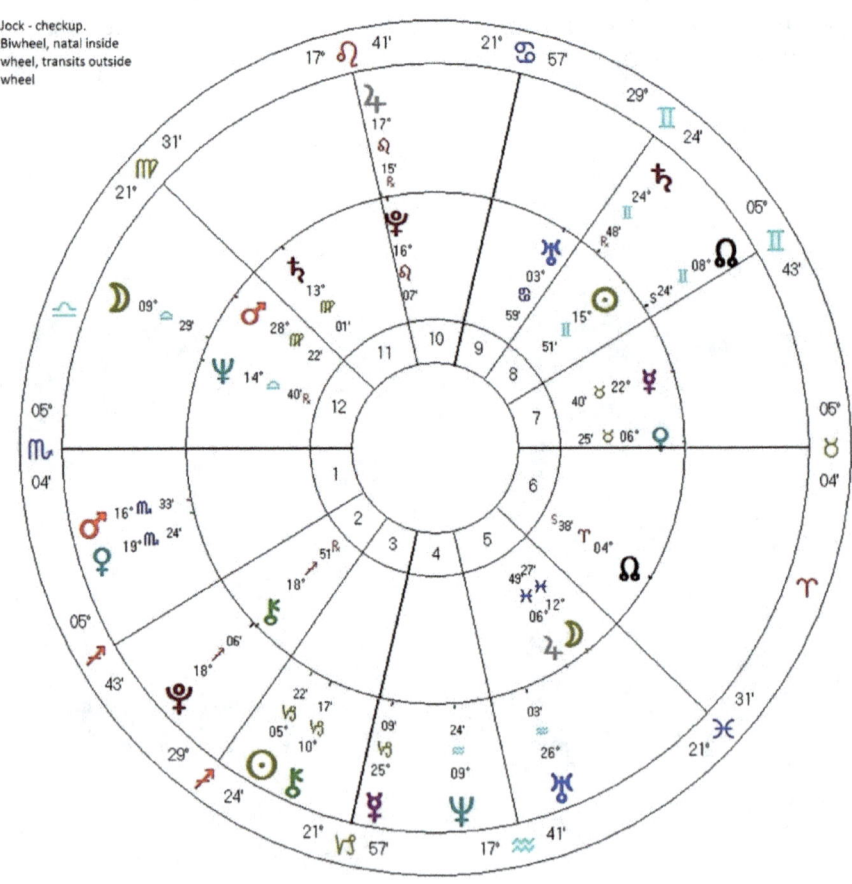

Chart: Jock - *birth chart inside wheel, outside wheel is his* **six-week radiation treatment** *for prostate cancer. What will happen, what is his prognosis for this operation?*

We can see that Tr Pluto is separating opposite Natal Sun, that's a good sign. It is conjunct Chiron, that is not so good, but both are Generational Planets and this shows a much better prospect than if it were a Luminary or an Inner Planet. Tr Jupiter is conjunct natal Pluto, not serious, both are Generational, but worth watching as it conjuncts his Midheaven. Tr Moon has passed its Full Moon position and is separating. All in all, it looks much better than his previous operation Transits and I would suggest to Jock to go ahead with his treatment. Update: He survived treatment and is alive and well.

Lesson 9

Noel: *Welcome to our final lesson.*

Student: Phew, we made it.

*N - So here we are at operations and other medical things. I gave you a lot of material in this last lesson. Some of it is useful, the rest is for your Christmas reading in the Appendixes. In summary, we always look for **conflict in the chart and focal Planets.** Looking at it holistically, we try to see **the whole chart, not single points.** Then we can use psychological foundations as the basis of ill health. We look at our focal Planets first, then look for triggers. If the psychological basis is triggered, then we have somatisation, which is an emotional or physical symptom of a psychological problem. Now for **Lychelle.***

S - We talked about her quite a bit last time. Her Moon didn't seem to be in too much trouble but it was part of a Fire Grand Trine with Pluto and Mercury/Jupiter.

N - Yes but is it the focal Planet? I would say it is one of many focal Planets.

S - Not in an obvious way. I think the Moon in that Fire Trine could represent a suppression of emotional needs. The Moon is in Sagittarius, a Sign that is not comfortable with "difficult" emotions. Jupiter in Aries certainly wants to keep everything "up" so maybe she is very spirited, perhaps overdoes the running around, doesn't get enough rest. Maybe when something is bothering her, she runs around more and takes less good care of herself. Sagittarius isn't a very health conscious Sign not until she has some kind of crash.

N - Very true and how does the Cardinal Grand Square affect her Fire Trine?

S - The high tension of the Square also keeps her running around, busy doing things and the tension spills over into the Grand Trine, which probably has to soak up the excess and perhaps that's what finally got to her Moon, i.e., her female organs.

N - Very good. This is holistic health astrology in action. I see the Grand Cross as contributing to denial. With the Grand Cross, she goes into denial and then the Fire Trine gives her the energy to run around to avoid real life situations that really need to be worked on. This is exactly what you said earlier. What events precipitated her ill health? What could be the triggers?

S - Pluto conjunct Moon, gawd.

N - *North Node opposite Moon and little Venus on Neptune?*

S - You think?

N - *Pluto definitely triggered issues. North Node is an indicator that this is a growth period for her... Some time ago, Lychelle had Chiron cross her Moon. See it in the 4th? This would have set off some bad vibes for her feminine organs and for her motherly and nurturing nature. She was perhaps challenged to nurture others or she might have felt that she was not being nurtured enough by her lover or mother or her children. So, the Chironic wound became suicidal, lonely, felt abandoned and betrayed. She believed that she was a nobody, on the trash pile. Pluto is good for this sort of thing.*

S - Yes indeed.

N - *She then spent quite some time looking for a good surgeon and getting professional medical advice. She is a very wise lady. Chiron made her aware of the weaknesses in her feminine system: mentally, emotionally and physically. Fortunately, he did come along and gave her enough warning before Pluto sowed his seeds of cancer. She was now quite prepared for the operation. North Node shows that she had learned heaps about herself, which she did by talking to doctors and others who went through the same procedure and illness. Also through talking to a counselor and other astrologers. The day of the operation, Pluto was moving forward. Separating at last. Venus was there energising Neptune with good feminine vibes.*

S - Aha!

N - *Neptune, who rules her lover and love life, is on the cusp of the 2nd (an Earth House), so it is good to have love under control and she felt loved when she went in for her operation. They found her womb was very diseased and her ovaries were also in a mess. A complete hysterectomy was necessary. The operation went perfectly with no post-trauma and she is currently looking for work and chats with me from time to time. I know that she is recovering very well.*

We have pre-trauma through Chiron. Then we have the wound being further traumatised by Pluto (heading towards cancer). Then we have the traumatising Planet (Pluto) separating, which is the best time for the operation. We have major lessons learned so that the illness won't come back through North Node.

S - Yay!

N - *Then we have the help of a little Inner Planet, just for that day: Venus. A nice gift from the Goddess.*

S - Trines aren't all they're cracked up to be.

N - *You bet. Next chart:* **Nev**.

S - Bundle-y fella! That means he has a tight chart.

N - *Natal Chiron on the Ascendant, the fundamental wound, often comes out as a sensory weakness.*

Eyes, ears, touch, etc. His weakness was vision and this chart shows his visit for surgery to correct it. First operation was a failure. Transiting Neptune applying leads to unfinished business. Transiting Jupiter was not finished, either, but he is secondary to Neptune. Nev's next chart is the success story. Transiting Neptune had crossed over the Ascendant for the six or so months it took to heal from the first operation and that made all the difference. There were no problems, a perfect result. No side effects and now he can see! Anything else? Look at the chart: North Node conjunct Mercury is sensory stuff.

S - I see Jupiter just passed opposite the Moon.

N - *Yes but separating and an old Transit. It would not affect the operation. Transiting Sun Trine Natal Sun, Transiting Pluto separating Square Mercury. Pluto is Retrograde so doesn't affect too much. Transiting Neptune is separating the Ascendant and Chiron, while Venus is separating opposite Mercury but wouldn't have affected the operation as it travels so fast. Next chart is his nose operation. Uranus opposite Sun is separating, so although it is a tough aspect it may just indicate a fast operation - in and out the same day. It may also show a stressful time but easing.*

S - Oh this is a planned surgery that hasn't happened yet?

N - *Yes, he is not too worried by it but would like your professional opinion madam astrologer. Actually, he gets two weeks off work* before the Christmas holidays. Jupiter conjunct Venus is a nice one and it is applying which may actually be positive.

S - Wow! Yes I saw that, no Moon aspects and no Full or New Moon which is good. Also Sun and Pluto are approaching a Trine to Venus.

N - *Oh, I didn't see that, no Mars aspects so bleeding minimal.*

S - Yes.

N - *Chiron Trine Mercury, applying, mmmm, from the 12th? No hidden problems? It's separating, just, so it should be OK. Neptune is quincunx Mercury which is separating, too, so minimal infection. Thus a summary would be?*

S - Sounds like it should go okay.

N - *Thanks doc! (Note: operation went exactly as described above, painful, in and out the same day, no problem with recovery)*

*Ok next chart: **Tara.** This is a nasty one. An emergency caesarean and she nearly bled to death giving birth.*

S - There's Mars just past Ascendant, perhaps signifying the surgery. Transiting Pluto T-Square the Chiron-Uranus Opposition.

N - *One basic astrology rule here: how sure are we of an accurate birth time? Mars could be applying, so we need to be aware of this Mars - Ascendant Transit.*

S - Right, hmm, does she have a transiting Yod? Tr Sun to Neptune-Pluto. Looks like it.

N - *Ooh, yes, you are right.*

S - Those can be nasty.

N - *It is not a very tight Transit but it is there. May have a 'building up' effect on the birth but the Finger of God can also be a good pattern. Childbirth may also be shown with her Transiting Moon trine Natal Moon. A Lunation effect with the Yod. Chiron Trine Moon maybe wound open too fast. It is a separating aspect but it will turn into an applying one soon. Some interesting features in this chart. I think the haemorrhaging is Mars. What do you think?*

S - That's possible. She was just about to have her Jupiter return. Those are usually positive, no?

N - *Should be and I've not really seen any bad ones: Jupiter Return might add intensity, a 'more of' like more blood. Chiron Trine Moon may be nasty, too, though the major trigger appears to be Mars. Otherwise, it would have been an easier birth: no Full or New Moons to worry about either. Mars is blood and there was lots of it.*

Next chart, **Jock:** *Natally, Scorpio Ascendant; active Pluto at the top of his chart; some heavy stuff here with Chiron as the focal point of a T-Square from Moon and Saturn. Hidden healing and perhaps unable to tap into his own healing potential. Mars is on the 12th House cusp. The next chart is his* **first operation for Prostate cancer** *which was a very aggressive and fast moving cancer. Both Transiting Pluto and Transiting Chiron are applying to oppose his Natal Sun. This is critical and not very positive for the operation or recovery as they are applying. Two days after a New Moon which is not bad.*

S - Yeesh.

N - *He had his Solar Return next day. Venus was applying, so some help there. Notice that the 6th House shows nothing. I mean doing nothing in all the charts we looked at so far.*

S - Um, no?

N - *The 6th hasn't come up much at all.*

S - Oh, right, I didn't understand.

N - *So much for the 6th House as health indicators.*

S - Yes. Noel Tyl said in his book on illness that it's not the 6th, it's the 12th and 1st and their rulers, etc.

N - *He's pretty much right. Next chart, Jock's coming* **radiotherapy.** *I think it goes for six weeks. Prognosis? It hasn't happened yet.*

S - Okay, one second. To do this right, I'd need to sit with the ephemeris and all but I'm glad that Mars is past the Square to Pluto. However, it is approaching an Opposition to Mercury, the ruler of the 12th. Transiting Pluto is approaching Conjunction to Chiron. That one I really don't like. Uranus is also heading to a quincunx with Mars.

N - *Exactly. Remember to keep orbs tight for an operation but wide enough for recovery time. And wide enough for the build-up (opening the wound) of the problem in the first place.*

S - Transiting Chiron is approaching a Square to Neptune but I don't know how soon that will happen. Fortunately Saturn is Retrograde, moving away from Square to natal Saturn for now. I think it could be problematic.

N - *Let's summarise Jock. He has already had one operation for prostate cancer 18 months ago and it came back. The doctors resorted to radiation because nothing else worked. His aspects for this date, the beginning of his radiation therapy, look fine. Except that we need to watch the Lord of his Chart: Transiting Pluto conjunct Natal Chiron. Both were implicated in his first operation and may have been the trigger for the prostate cancer in the first place. So, although the therapy goes well, there will remain unfinished business relating to Pluto and Chiron.*

S - He was having his Chiron Return. Those Chiron Transits can be unpleasant.

N - *You bet, a whole new cycle, 56 years of it. It's all about wounds to his genitals.*

S - Life ain't a picnic.

N - *So I would say that he will survive treatment but not have as much comfort in this operation as he would like (Postscript: he survived treatment and has had a few health frights since).*

S - He can't depend on the doctors alone to save him. He's got to make lifestyle and other changes.

N - *Yes. Pluto and Chiron are two bad dudes and his Sun is losing its light.*

S - What does that mean: Sun is losing its light?

N - *Sun is opposed by both transiting Pluto and Chiron, which clouds it over. Sun is vitality, so with so little vitality he has little 'life' or in my words 'light' to shine.*

S - So Pluto is now approaching Square to my Sun.

N - *Yes?*

S - Am I next?

N - *We don't have your chart, so can't tell.*

S - Could I email you? I'd be interested in your assessment.

N - *What are your details, that is if you really want us to look at it? We can do it now? Or later, it's up to you.*

S - I've had some ongoing health issues, plus enormous emotional stress. I'd like to do it privately, if that's okay.

N - *Of course, email me and we will do some magic.*

S - Thank you!

N - *No worries. But you are under stress, of course. Look at Pluto and Neptune both are powerfully placed in your chart. So you need to talk to them. I love doing that in my meditations.*

Summary for operations: watch out for Neptune, Pluto, Chiron and Mars and especially Saturn for recovery; Uranus for fast events and convalescence. This can be indicated by looking at what comes along over the next few weeks while they recover. Also it is good to look at Transits heading up to the illness or operation. This gives a good picture of what is underlying the issues. Last but not least, consider the emotional picture.

Well, Student, how are you feeling about astrological healing?

S - I think this course has been terrific.

N - *Thank you. My approach is from Taoism / astrology / psychology and I seek to locate dramatic events in clients with Transits, particularly Conjunctions and Oppositions.*

S - Can you give sources for the way you approach things? You mentioned Arroyo but I don't think he talks about health issues in his book on the Elements. I've got all his books.

N - *Arroyo did say look for 'conflict' and that is what I took from him but what a revelation for me that single word was. From conflict, I went to Liz Greene, who gave me more insight about the Elements and I put them together from my interactions with my counseling and astrology clients.*

I suppose it's also from all the time writing lesson notes for my courses on Taoism and Psychological Astrology that helped me formulate my thoughts. I also use my understanding of Taoist and

Chinese healing and how the organs in the body will help each other when one is having trouble. That is very holistic, which is very important. When one organ runs down, the others will give of themselves to support the sick organ system. This means that we don't always have the weakest organ as the sick organ, not at all. It could be the one pumping harder than the rest when we read pulses. We find that some organ systems are weak and some are strong but the feeble ones are not always weak. They may just be giving some of their energy to the one pumping hardest so that it is not falling apart. Our equilibrium will last longer when all systems help each other. When the most obvious looks to be the real problem, we must always look deeper to find out exactly what is happening. Then we have the emotional basis for the illness. Many time, I see people with emotional issues associated with physical illness and I try to put one and one together. Sometimes, I get three and other times I get two. Astrology is the focus of all my life's work put into practice, this is my health philosophy.

Warning: always seek professional medical advice for any health complaints, particularly for children.

Appendix 1

Common Defence Mechanisms

Defence mechanisms are programs that run silently and deeply within your unconscious to protect you from harmful memories and sensations. You are generally completely unaware of them. The term 'defence' explains how important they are to your self preservation. When a situation arises that upsets your emotional stability, a defence mechanism is initiated to shut it down. This protects you from experiencing unpleasant feelings and thoughts. It is not a cure, it is more a means to band-aid the problem until you are ready to deal with its underlying cause.

Denial: You ignore or reject the real situation when you find it too difficult or painful to accept something, *"I don't mind at all that you are working with your ex-wife!"*

Rationalization: You come up with excuses to justify your decisions. *"I can't focus on this new exercise program. I might injure my shoulder and then I can't play bowls."*

Intellectualization: A form of rationalisation but more towards the intellectual end of the spectrum. *"My inability to confront my affect failings is a form of intellectual rationalisation."*

Isolation of affect: You are able to intellectualise but not feel the emotion. *"My friend died in a car crash yesterday, I am sure I will miss him. What's for dinner tonight?"*

Reaction Formation: You act in the opposite direction to what you really feel. This happens for instance when you don't like something but don't know how to cope with the consequences of expressing it, *"Wow, a pencil sharpener, what a thoughtful gift, I just love it, just what I needed."*

Projection: You dump onto others what you find unacceptable within yourself. *"I think about cheating on you, so you must be cheating on me."*

Displacement: You redirect your feelings onto someone else or some other object. For instance, instead of confronting a difficult workmate, you take it out on your partner when you get home, *"I can't stand you!"*

Suppression: You defend against your thoughts or feelings about a situation. You push it down so you don't feel it. This is the only conscious defence mechanism. *"I will just keep doing what I am doing and I am sure I will just get over it."*

Regression: You revert back to a previous childhood stage, rather than confront current reality. *"I won't give up my safe, old pillow. I can't fall asleep without it."*

Sublimation: You redirect unacceptable feelings or urges so that they are socially acceptable. *"I just got a job in the prison system, you should see all those angry people, I am really going to enjoy working there."*

Defenses are how we manage our unconscious urges, instincts and drives. They are how we hold back our inner dragons. It doesn't free them from their prisons and it doesn't heal them. It merely binds them with a ball and chain to stop them running amok and disturbing our life.

Appendix 2

Article: Miracle Healing

As an astrologer, I am often asked to provide information on a person's constitutional health. By 'constitutional health' I mean the inherited physical strengths and weaknesses of an individual. For instance a new-born baby will have specific strengths and weaknesses inherited from her mother and father and from previous generations. She will be sensitive with allergies for instance, or have weak lungs, which are sometimes obvious in the birth chart.

Astrologers are sometimes called upon to tell the time of someone's death, too. Gale was an astrologer herself and asked me when her chart suggested she would pass away. She had cancer and was told she didn't have long to live. She wanted to prepare herself and her family for the sad but inevitable event.

"When will I die?" she asked me.

Normally, I don't do this sort of thing, but for Gale, a realist and an astrologer friend, I told her that I saw little in her chart other than transition, change from one opportunity to another. She then asked me to draw up the charts of her husband and grown children. Their charts all pointed to a loss in October, just when her own changes appeared, and, incidentally, when she passed away.

Apart from astrology, sometimes it is possible to 'know' the answer to a problem through other channels. Sure, astrology is one means to an answer but dowsing is another and this is where people like Harald Tietze, Peter Ruehmkorff and Frank Moody come into their own.

Frank once dowsed the blood clot of a patient in hospital a thousand miles away using his pendulum. Harald uses his rods and body sensitivity to find healthy rooms in a person's home and to warn owners to be wary of high 'Earth Radiation' areas or negative ley lines.

My dowser friend, Peter Ruehmkorff, once helped a lady who had very serious health problems. She said that she had been feeling extremely unwell for some months. She and her doctors couldn't find a cause for her ill health and none of the medications or remedies worked. She was becoming more and more fatigued each day and she was becoming frightened.

When Peter arrived at the lady's house, he went from room to room with his pendulum and rods, but could detect no Earth rays, no entities, no indications of 'other' possible causes. There were no reasons that he could find for her deteriorating health.

So, in desperation, he got out his 'electromagnetic field detector' to see if there were any highly dangerous electrical fields present, but again, nothing. Peter sat down at her kitchen table to contemplate for a while... and then returned to his car.

Fortunately for this lady, she had called the only dowser in the world who carries a Geiger Counter in his tool box.

He was directed straight to her bedroom where, immediately over the centre of her bed, the Geiger Counter went crazy. He found a long stick and lifted the bed covers up and there, under her bed, was a cardboard box. Inside that cardboard box were some rocks, and they were highly radioactive.

The lady's son had been for a holiday to Rum Jungle, uranium country in the Northern Territory of Australia, and had found some nice looking rocks for his collection. When he arrived home in Sydney he asked his mother to look after his rock collection for a while.

These deadly 'rocks' now safely reside at Sydney University as test specimens in the physics laboratory. Miracle? No, just damn good scientific luck and an incredible dowser.

One more example of extraordinary healing happened when I participated in a meditation group some years ago. After the meditation, we decided to do some hands-on healing with each other while the energy was still strong. Someone in the group could relax only so far during meditation before he would gag and choke and come back to consciousness. I practiced hands-on healing back in those days, so I thought I would try to help him.

I put my hands on his head and moved them around his back and neck as I relaxed and went into a light trance. I got the feeling that 'sand' and 'beach' were involved with his problem. I said to him:

"Beach, you're at the beach and there is sand, lots of sand and you need to yell and scream... yes, it's the sand, I see lots of it, it has something to do with sand."

I wasn't really sure what had happened to him but the word 'sand' came up again and again. Moments later, he jumped up out of the chair and vomited in the bathroom.

When he came, back he explained that he now remembered an episode when he was a 10-year-old child playing with a boy at the beach. He didn't know this boy but he was happy to play with anyone, he was lonely. Soon afterward, the boy began hitting him, he couldn't remember why, but he remembered being forced face down into the sand, trying to scream for help. That's when this boy began to shovel sand into his mouth to stop him screaming. The next thing that he remembered he was waking up in the hospital. He had forgotten this incident completely. After this, he could meditate without gagging and choking.

People call them 'miracles' but in truth they are answers received by 'extraordinary' means. To many, it is a miracle, but for those who do this, it is part of their daily life.

Appendix 3

Article: Amazing Experiences In Trance with the astrological Archetypes

Astrologers do lots of things other than astrology readings, some of us are therapists and healers. We draw upon our many skills to enhance the art of astrology and bring about change and transformation in our client's lives. This article describes how a multidimensional approach to healing drawing upon astrology, meditation and self-hypnosis can bring about spiritual growth.

At a workshop I presented some years ago, I guided the group to meditate on astrological archetypes. Archetypes are symbols. In this case, we used astrological symbols, which represent various aspects of our personality, strengths and weaknesses. By contacting specific archetypes, you can gain insight about yourself which might aid you in your journey of healing and spiritual development.

I have Saturn and Jupiter in an uncomfortable aspect (Square) with each other. At this workshop, I went into trance and saw my own chart laid out before me. I looked around and wondered who I could work with this. I looked at Pluto, nah, not him again, then I looked at my 7th House, and there was Jupiter, frozen like an icicle.

Moving my gaze, I saw Saturn, the Lord of the Chart, standing smug in the 10th House. Ah ha! The lights came on for me as I realised what had happened. Powerful Saturn had pointed his finger at Jupiter and froze him to keep him quiet, just like Mr Freeze in Batman.

At this time in my life, I was working very hard, I needed every second and every ounce of energy for my work and university studies. Any distraction was a burden and Jupiter was in the habit of drawing troublesome situations into my life - fun situations that took precious time and energy away from my career and studies.

Jupiter just wanted to have fun with my wife and kids, they wanted their dad back. But I was focused on career and Saturn is the archetype responsible for achieving my goals. I loved achieving and being successful and had given Saturn free reign over my life to provide a career and purpose in life. However, Saturn took his role too seriously and wouldn't allow me to be distracted from working towards these goals.

Saturn was stronger than Jupiter and dominated him, sometimes severely. Jupiter wanted to have fun but Saturn wanted him to keep quiet so that he could get on with building my career. Each archetype has a need to be expressed and Jupiter, like a child, would not stay quiet for long. When he had thawed, he would break out and cause mischief and Saturn would then freeze him up again.

I looked at Jupiter, he is good friends with my Venus who stands next to him, but Venus had turned away and was ignoring him completely. I knew why, Jupiter was a boring icicle.

This was a real problem for me. Both Venus and Jupiter were involved in drawing people to me, my clients, colleagues and friends. Without them I would be a shell, successful academically but not in life. I had to do something about this, now.

Still in a light trance I went over to Saturn and asked him to *'help me out here.'* I explained that he was hurting me and that he had to ease off. I brought Jupiter over, he was not happy. Jupiter was angry with Saturn. He knew he had little say in the matter but all the same, Jupiter wanted some respect from Saturn, the 'Lord of the Chart'.

I had to explain to the two of them that their disharmony was affecting me. I decided to come up with some suitable options. Jupiter agreed to tone down his demands for play and Saturn to ease up on his work-load and self-discipline. They agreed, though I could see that neither trusted the other.

I check up on them when I think about it and often I notice Jupiter frozen like a statue, and I have to get them back together. But on the whole, it has made a marked change in my life.

Having just typed this paragraph I meditated on my chart again. Saturn was in black, as he always is for me, and he was wearing white gloves. He sees himself as a conductor, an artist, he is so proud of the work we have done together. I owe him recognition for my motivation and determination after placing myself under enormous pressure to complete the work I set myself.

I looked across for Jupiter and saw Saturn bringing him over to me. He was guiltily dusting Jupiter down like he were a dusty old coat. Oh dear, at least Saturn had not frozen him this time. I noticed that Jupiter had been locked in the closet.

When I was going through another tough time, Neptune Transited slowly across my Capricorn Ascendant. I went 'inside' my chart to see what was happening in my inner world. I looked across at my Ascendant and there before me was a huge rocky mountain with barren and dusty planes surrounding it. Oh, not very good, but it did describe how I was feeling: barren.

Capricorn, my Ascendant, is represented by a goat climbing the mountain, so it was an appropriate image. I dropped in to see Chiron who was living in a cave opposite the mountain on the other side of the river. Chiron looked rather primitive, quite unevolved. So I spent some time working with him to speed his evolution.

Chiron changed rapidly with each meditation. He soon learned tai chi and began manifesting his energy within me. Chiron quickly became my inner Taoist and we would meditate together beside his fire, inside his cave.

I noticed that below the mountain was a river of muddy water. That was transiting Neptune, who had begun to cross my Capricorn Ascendant. He was trying to create flow and harmony in my life by eroding my ingrained bad habits, values and attitudes. Neptune was devastating, he washed away stale belief systems and undermined my self-esteem. He made me change by drowning me in my own strength.

You see, Capricorn is strength, he is inflexible and he is disciplined. I was dominated by these earthy characteristics with a strong Saturn, the ruler of Capricorn and the Lord Of The Chart. I was not flowing in my daily life. Neptune came along and washed these bad habits away whether I liked it or not. He was ruthless and I was devastated for some 12 months.

Each time I went into trance to see what was happening I saw a wonderful panorama being created right before my eyes. The mountain was no longer so rugged and barren. Below it, I saw a clean river, green foliage grew on the river banks. As each meditation proceeded, I witnessed the change in myself and the change in my inner world. I worked with the archetypes, I asked them to help me cope with the stresses I was undergoing and I tried to follow their advice. It was a cooperative period of growth through hardship and change.

This morning I meditated before rising, it's a good time for me. I went to see how my Ascendant was going and dropped in to visit

Chiron. Chiron was standing outside his cave dressed in his flowing blue gown as he does now. He smiled and began to chuckle when he saw me, he patted the top of my head and said, *"All gone, all gone"*. I actually felt his hand patting me, this almost brought me back out of trance. Then I realised what he was saying. I had no hair, two days ago I cut it off on a whim, the very first time I have ever had short hair, I looked bald. He was laughing. Well, well, these archetypes certainly have personality.

The very first time I tried the archetype meditation in my practice, I was fortunate to have a very talented client to work with. Dana came for help because she had died many times and wanted it to stop. She had asthma since she was a child, so bad that she had been rushed off to hospital on many occasions. Now she had small children and wanted to be healed. I suggested that we work with the archetypes in trance.

At the first session, Dana met the Sun; he came to her as an African in a lion skin toga. She asked why he wore a toga and he replied, *"Because it's cool."* I was impressed, humour indeed. This lady experienced many interesting things in trance and was a dream to work with.

Dana met her Cancer archetype but couldn't understand what was said, Cancer spoke very softly. Dana asked the Sun to tell her what Cancer was saying. The Sun told her that Cancer said something that Dana didn't want to hear. Dana then told Cancer to speak up even if she herself didn't want to hear it. Dana was silent for some moments and finally told me that Cancer said that she was intolerant and judgmental. Dana was a therapist too.

We worked once with Jesus. I must admit that I suggested this because I had had success with another client the week before. Jesus told her that she had asthma because her parents were always on the brink of divorce. She would become ill to keep them together. This was almost too much for Dana, she came back quiet and pale, and she told me that this was true. Having heard this explanation, she realised just how true it was. Jesus gave her a feather and told her to *'walk gently, walk softly'*.

In the final few sessions, she got in touch with her health archetypes; they told her she should be doing the Taoist chi breathing exercises I had taught her. She told them that she didn't have time, she had two small children and she worked hard each day. They told her that they would wake her up in the middle of the night to do it. They did, and this terrified her so much that she stopped the meditations.

Another lady, Amanda, had Saturn in her 1st House and Jupiter in her 12th. On one occasion, Jupiter invited her to visit his castle, she agreed. When she arrived, she saw a magical well that would drop her into her deep subconscious if she touched its water. She was tempted when Jupiter told her that the well contained all her wishes and dreams.

She then saw his magnificent castle, but behind its stone wall stood a huge three headed dragon and he was frightening. Jupiter turned to her and handed her a plastic sword and shield then said *"Go and fight the dragon."* Amanda was horrified, no way! Jupiter then said, *"Go on, you do it all the time."*

At that moment Amanda realised that the dragon represented her mother whom she fought with all the time. She could never win because she didn't have the 'weapons' to win with. She looked at the dragon and saw words spelled out beside it, 'Guilt', 'Pain', 'Fear'. Ash, just how her mother made her feel.

During our trance sessions together, Amanda went on to visit other archetypes such as Saturn, who had all of her certificates and diplomas on his walls. He explained that he did all that for her. Sagittarius was also an archetype that she had to visit; he wanted her to study, study, and study. He had to be told that if she did that she would never produce anything, she would be studying forever. This was one of her major stumbling blocks. She was an astrologer, too, but she didn't think that she would ever know enough to be able to go out and practice. Her stumbling blocks were there in her astrological chart, and in her meditations.

The insights that we gain using the trance state and astrological archetypes from our personal horoscope can pave the way for inner healing, the most powerful form of healing available to us.

Appendix 4

Inflammation and the Four Elements

Inflammation is considered by many health authorities to be one of the leading causes of our 21st Century health crisis. I will carry out a brief examination of what may be Elemental inflammatory triggers. Inflammation arises when tissues become either mechanically or biochemically inflamed and irritated. Long-term inflammation can lead to organ degeneration and disease. The dominant Elements within the natal chart can show our susceptibility to inflammation.

Fire: this is an obvious choice for the most susceptible Element for inflammation. Fire is particularly associated with physical activity, excitement, sexual arousal, sports injuries and burnout from excessive partying, sexual activity, alcohol and drug use. Look for a dominance in Aries, Leo and Sagittarius; the 1st, 5th and 9th Houses; the Luminaries in these Signs and Houses; Conjunctions of Sun, Mars and Jupiter to the Angles and to the Luminaries. In these cases, you would seek such herbs, vitamins and minerals that reduce inflammation. Lots of water to drink and play in, cooling herbs and foods are a good place to start.

Air: this would stem from excessive intellectual activity including headaches, racing negative thoughts, anxiety, stress, worry and disturbed sleep: all of which are top contenders for illness in the western world. Air Signs often seek relief from stressful thinking by excessive drinking and drug abuse. This is not the sensation seeking of the Fire Signs but is directed towards alleviating excessive intellectual or mental activity. Air Signs use it to calm down their racing mind while Fire Signs use it to become even more physically excited and stimulated. Look for a dominance in Gemini, Libra and Aquarius; the 3rd, 7th and 11th Houses; the Luminaries in these Signs and Houses; plus Conjunctions of Mercury, Venus and Uranus to the Angles and Luminaries.

Earth: this too points towards physical illness and inflammation, though we would direct this understanding towards the bowels, stomach and guts - problems with assimilation and elimination. We could say that this issue is again a typical western health problem caused by over-eating and over-consumption Look for a dominance in Taurus, Virgo and Capricorn; the 2nd, 6th and 10th Houses; the Luminaries in these Signs and Houses; plus

Conjunctions of Mercury, Venus and Sagittarius to the Angles and Luminaries.

Water: here we would consider such stressful activities as relationship troubles triggering sadness, depression. Also, extreme over-sensitivity to other people's problems. Inflammatory health issues may involve the sexual organs, fevers, excessive fluid build-up, fatigue, lack of exercise, excessive sitting and sleeping. On the psychological plane, this could mean spiritual identity and existential crises, issues with self-esteem and self-worth, weight problems, etc. Look for a dominance in Cancer, Scorpio and Pisces; the 4th, 8th and 12th Houses; the Luminaries in these Signs and Houses; plus Conjunctions of Moon, Pluto and Neptune to the Angles and Luminaries.

Anti-inflammatory herbs and natural remedies abound in nature, look around in your fresh produce stores and health-food stores. Seek them out, talk to your health professionals and learn about good health practices.

Appendix 5

Recommended Reading List

The Combination of Stellar Influences - R. Ebertin

Therapeutic Astrology - Greg Bogart

Relating: An Astrological Guide to Living With Others on a Small Planet - Liz Greene

Astrology, Karma & Transformation: The Inner Dimensions of the Birth Chart - Stephen Arroyo

Astrology, Psychology and the Four Elements - Stephen Arroyo

The Gods of Change: Pain, Crisis and the Transits of Uranus, Neptune and Pluto (Arkana's Contemporary Astrology Series) - Howard Sasportas

Exploring Consciousness in the Horoscope - Noel Tyl

The Health Zodiac: A Practical Guide to Understanding Your Health Cycles Through Astrology - Pamela Rowe

Planetary Heredity - Michel Gauquelin

Astrology for Women: Roles & Relationships - Gloria Star

Fit for Life II: Living Health - Harvey and Marilyn Diamond

Fire Your Doctor - Dr Andrew Saul

Barriers & Boundaries - Liz Greene

A Handbook of Astrology for Australia and New Zealand - Jane Bennet and Craig McIntosh

Psychological Astrology and The Twelve Houses - Noel Eastwood

The Miracle of MSM - Stanley Jacob

The Miracle Mineral Solution of the 21st Century - Jim Humble

Kombucha Miracle Fungus - Harald Tietze

Appendix 6

Inflammatory Illness

In Search of a Germ Theory Equivalent for Chronic Disease -
Garry Egger, PhD, MPH

Prevention Chronic Disease 2012;9:110301. DOI: Center For Disease Control and Prevention.

Abstract: The fight against infectious disease advanced dramatically with the consolidation of the germ theory in the 19th century. This focus on a predominant cause of infections (i.e., microbial pathogens) ultimately led to medical and public health advances (e.g., immunization, pasteurization, antibiotics). However, the resulting declines in infections in the 20th century were matched by a rise in chronic, noncommunicable diseases, for which there is no single underlying aetiology. The discovery of a form of low-grade systemic and chronic inflammation ("metaflammation"), linked to inducers (broadly termed "anthropogens") associated with modern man-made environments and lifestyles, suggests an underlying basis for chronic disease that could provide a 21st century equivalent of the germ theory...

Inflammation and Disease

For more than 2,000 years, classical inflammation has been recognized by the symptoms identified by the Roman physician Aurelius Celsus as pain (*dolor*), redness (*rubor*), heat (*calor*), and swelling (*tumor*), with the more recent addition of loss of function (*torpor*). This form of classical inflammation is typically a short-term response to infection and injury, aimed at removing the infective stimulus and allowing repair of the damaged tissue, ultimately resulting in healing and a return to homeostasis. However, in 1993, researchers discovered a different type of prolonged, dysregulated, and maladaptive inflammatory response associated with obesity, which they suggested may explain the disease-causing effects of excessive weight gain (6). "Metaflammation" (9), as it was later called because of its link with the metabolic system, differs from classical inflammation in that it 1) is low-grade, causing only a small rise in immune system markers (i.e., a 4- to 6-fold increase vs a several-hundred-fold increase); 2) is persistent and results in chronic, rather than acute, allostasis; 3) has systemic rather than local effects; 4) has antigens that are less apparent as foreign agents or microbial pathogens and, hence, have been referred to as "inducers"; 5) appears to perpetuate, rather than resolve disease; and 6) is associated with a reduced, rather than increased, metabolic rate...

Please read the rest of Dr Garry Egger's article here:

Link: www.cdc.gov/pcd/issues/2012/11_0301.htm

About Noel Eastwood

Noel Eastwood is a retired psychologist who has studied and taught psychotherapy, tai chi and Taoist meditation, astrology and the tarot for more than 30 years. He is also the author of: *Psychological Astrology and the Twelve Houses*. Pluto's Cave is a metaphor for the hidden world of the unconscious.

Dragons are those invisible yet powerful urges that drive us in predetermined ways. They come from our deep unconscious when we are fearful, angry, sad or uncertain. Dragons can be trained to fly and rejoice in their power, yet few initiates know how to do this.

Inner Selves are parts of our psyche splintered off when bad things happen. These, too, live inside our Cave, our deep Unconscious. They feed our dragons when something triggers unpleasant memories.

Wishing Wells are our treasures, those wondrous potentials that lie hidden deep within. For most, they remain untouched throughout an entire lifetime.

Entering Pluto's Cave is a journey into the unconscious for those who seek to tame their inner Dragons.

In ancient mystery schools, the term 'initiate' is often used to describe the seeker of knowledge. Their quest is to find and rescue, support and nurture their own injured inner self. As many issues arise from childhood traumas, initiates realise that the dragon is in fact their fears. They develop strategies to manage the issues that held them back in life and stunted their relationships. The traumas of the past can indeed be healed.

Initiates delve into 'magic wishing wells' of the mind, places of discovery and wonder. They learn meditation techniques that have been practised for centuries to control fears and emotions. They dip into these wells to learn more about the meaning of life.

Why not join Noel in your own adventure to uncover your potential?

For more information please visit: **www.plutoscave.com**

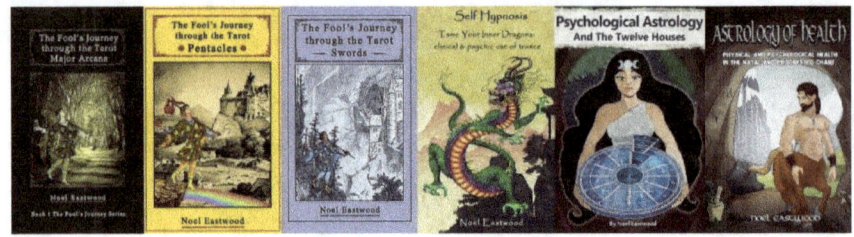

Endnotes

[1] In this book, I use the term "Outer Planets" to include Jupiter, Saturn, Uranus, Neptune and Pluto.

www.ingramcontent.com/pod-product-compliance
Lightning Source LLC
Chambersburg PA
CBHW071909290426
44110CB00013B/1335